Blokes
& SHEDS

Blokes & SHEDS

TEXT BY

JIM HOPKINS

PHOTOGRAPHY BY

JULIE RILEY

 HarperCollins*Publishers New Zealand Limited*

With thanks to shed pioneer Mark Thomson, author of *Blokes & Sheds*
(published by Angus & Robertson, Australia).

Published in association with

First published 1998

Reprinted 1998

HarperCollins*Publishers (New Zealand) Limited*
P.O. Box 1, Auckland

Text copyright © Jim Hopkins, 1998
Photographs copyright © Julie Riley, 1998

Jim Hopkins and Julie Riley assert the moral right to be
identified as the authors of this work.

ISBN 1 86950 278 7

Designed by Jan Harris
Typeset by Pauline Whimp
Printed by Griffin Press, Australia

Acknowledgements

Heartfelt thanks to all the people who wrote to us, rang us, welcomed us and shared their sheds. To those who didn't sneak into this volume, don't worry, we'll be back. Thanks to John Paul and the team from Skyline Garages for their talent-spotting, their contacts and their support. And thanks to Ian and Sue at HarperCollins for their guidance, patience and all-round literary genius (grovel, grovel!). Apologies to Tess for monopolising the only table in the house, and to Tom as well for spending so much time in other people's sheds. Thanks too, to Tess for her wise guidance and excellent advice and for acting as a go-between and buffer zone. Special thanks to Stephen Goodenough, who did such a wonderful job printing the photographs in this book, and to Vickie Piper, for taking the photograph of Julie. And finally, thanks to everyone with a shed, just for having one. And apologies to all those with fantastic sheds we never even heard about but doubtless will now.

P.S. Thanks to the lady in the lonely farmhouse in Hawke's Bay who took in two wayfarers and provided the all-important petroleum out of which they had unhappily run.

Jim Hopkins and Julie Riley

Introduction

Everybody's got a shed story. And everybody wants to tell it. Mention the subject and people wake up, light up and the tales spill out, like kids from a class at the end of term. There's no Gospel According to the Expert, you see, in the matter of sheds. No one's told us what to think. And no one's told us what to say to escape the cool disdain of Those Who Know.

This is rare in an age much inclined to analyse and stigmatise. Yet, somehow, the shed has got off scot-free. At a time when most matters masculine are under the judgmental microscope (and not doing too well) the great refuge of blokedom has just sort of sat there, out the back, pretty much unnoticed. The fact that sheds have escaped the scrutiny of those with fingers to wag and tuts to tut is really quite surprising.

There can be no doubt blokes have had a bad press of late. As one who is, for better or worse, of the bloke persuasion, I'll freely concede there will be those who say we had it coming. And they may well be right. We know that, for centuries, a motley assortment of patriarchs were busily devoted to the oppression of just about anyone who came into view. But, for the confused regiments of modern-day blokes who have never consciously patriarchally oppressed anybody, the condemnation has all been rather disorienting and disheartening.

We've had to come to terms with an oft-orchestrated litany of shortcomings, defects, failings and flaws. We've discovered that we're lousy fathers, lousy husbands and, in the evenings when we're not being either, we still find time (although never enough) to be lousy lovers. We've had to come to terms with being emotionally cold, excessively aggressive, unhealthily sexist and rather prone to dying sooner than we should. We're the new noxious pests – an endangering species even. Poised on the cusp of the millennium, masculinity is a downright liability. The best thing we could do, it would seem, is leave our modest contribution to the survival of the species in a jar and toddle off to a home for the terminally redundant.

So pervasive is this view that the next sentence will read as outright heresy, but we'll give it a go. Blokes are creative, generous, energetic and passionate. Blokes care. Maybe not about the things therapists and counsellors and relationship gurus think they should, but get them out in the shed and it's a different story. The only things blokes bottle up out there are assorted nails and screws that 'may come in handy one day'. Give a bloke a shed and all his life-enhancing qualities come hurtling to the fore. And if they're not heading in the direction the psychobabblers would wish, that may just be a fact of life. Something that won't change till the vast majority of us are pensioned off, replaced by well proportioned 'cyborgs', genetically engineered to remember birthdays and anniversaries.

The fact is, men define themselves by doing things. Now, anecdotal evidence is always dodgy, but I offer a recent sporting interview as a modicum of proof. In this interview, some Super 12 assistant coach or muscle memory coordinator affectionately described a first-five eight as having 'lovely hands'. He did not mean the gent in question had lovely hands. That kind of direct physical compliment would be viewed as unseemly. What he meant was that the player did lovely things with his hands, that he displayed great dexterity and skill. So, making a huge leap from the particular to the general, let's assert that, for blokes, doing is feeling. There are sound evolutionary reasons why this should be so, but I won't go into those. Let's just say this blokish trait has come in handy, at various times, along the Darwinian way. And is still coming in handy today, in sheds the length and breadth of the land.

You could argue there is, in fact, a clear link between the caveman and the shedman. Some years ago, sociologist Lionel Tiger suggested that the sports teams of today are direct descendants of the hunting parties and war parties of Neolithic times. And when you see someone win a cup and brandish it, double-handed, in the air in exultant triumph, as if it were the severed head of some slain adversary in a Conan movie, the thought occurs that he could be right. Given that the hunting of wildebeest and mammoths in built-up areas, not to mention the conquest of the neighbour and the appropriation of his rhubarb, do tend to be frowned upon, perhaps sport does offer a palatable outlet for these ancient impulses.

If that's so, I suspect the sheddies are the successors of the guys who were a bit too small or a bit slow to make the War Blacks. Maybe they'd been on the wrong end of a sabre-toothed tiger or something, so they hung around back at base, working on the Mark 3 slingshot, or ways to get the rectangles out of wheels. The alternative is that these tinkerers and tweakers, enhancers and improvers did sally forth with their peers but, at the end of a hard day skirmishing or hunting, they were the ones who felt compelled to shuffle down to the fissure at the back of the cave and design a spear that wouldn't bounce off the average mastodon's flanks. One way or the other, whether his work was done in lieu of or après-foray, *Shedus erectus* now has countless heirs. The world's potterers have benefitted much from his genetic legacy.

Before you dismiss this hypothesis as entirely fanciful, think of all the surnames that come from crafts and trades practised by and passed down through several generations. Or consider the significant number of shedmen we met whose fathers or grandfathers, or both, had been carpenters, or shipbuilders, or wheelwrights and to whom they attributed their love of working with their

hands. Maybe nature and nurture do come together in ways we still don't quite understand. One thing is clear to me, having seen dads with their sons in the shed, and that is that the biggest influence any father can have is no influence at all.

However, it would be wrong to pretend that the shed is entirely immune from controversy. A dark whiff of misogyny has hung about the shed for some time. It's best expressed by the shed storyteller who said, 'It's like the dog box. When it's too rough inside, you go out to the shed. You get left in peace. No nagging, no kids, no wife – they just get in the way.' It's not an easy position to defend, so I won't try. The best that can be said is that this aversion to others appears to be a passing phenomenon. And set against it are all the sheddies who chose to say, 'I suppose some men would have a shed to get away from the wife – but that's not true in my case.' Without exception, I believed them. Generally speaking, sheds seem to be part of a partnership and a lot of wives we talked to are very proud of the miracles wrought within their precincts, although they wanted that kept confidential.

It's also true that sheds are not a uniquely male bastion. I have several letters, some indignant and some angry, from shed-women who forcefully reject the proposition that their cherished sanctuary is actually part of a blokes-only zone. Let us accept then, that no thing is ever black and white and that the blokesses will have their day. Maybe in the sequel?

What sheds do, undeniably, represent is something about the way we want to be. Much is spoken these days of New Zealand identity. A lot of it is self-serving twaddle, an argument promoted by certain superior souls who want other people's money to pay for the things they enjoy doing. What they tend to overlook is that, apart from the unique, painful and evolving relationship between Maori and European, most of our 'identity' comes from somewhere else. Our religions, philosophy, notions of class and gender, our legal system, our political processes, our media style, planning concepts, even our fairy stories and notions of Father Christmas mainly come from somewhere else. We can't even claim to have invented a sport of our own.

What we have invented, or evolved – and it's often confused with identity – is an attitude, to the world and each other, that is ours and ours alone. If anything summed it up, it would probably be Ed Hillary's line after climbing Mt Everest, 'We knocked the bugger off.' Laconic and tongue-in-cheek, it treats the extraordinary as commonplace and makes it a team effort as well. That kind of

self-effacement is important here. We particularly dislike the growth hormone that can make some people too big for their boots. And we particularly like self-reliance, the willingness to 'give it a go'. Born of necessity, it survives by choice. Being willing to give it a go is expected, it's part of how we want to see ourselves, it's part of our attitude. Which is why sheds, and what they represent, are important. We've got our share of famous sheds. The one in which Richard Pearce built his aeroplanes. Or where the jet boat, the electric fence and the animal tranquiliser gun were developed. Then, of course, there's Rutherford's den (a sort of basement shed) where he first picked up a chisel and split the atom.

There's a tradition of ingenuity we enjoy and still discover out in the shed. We found sheds whose owners had built their own bulldozer to clear the section or were making Tesla generators to produce pollution-free propulsion. We found sheds where the old was being salvaged and the new created. What was in them may not be the stuff of pompous catalogues and earnest reviews, but that's probably the secret of their strength. They are the places where 'anything's possible', where you do what you want, not what you think you should.

I suspect it explains why sheds appeal and why people get such delight out of talking about them. I remember someone recalling 'the generations of things' that had accumulated in their shed. And someone else speculating about the role of climate and the effect of cold weather both on the need to invent and the evolution of the shed. And someone else, paradoxically, explaining how the word 'shed' is a corruption of 'shade' and that the first ones were a screening roof supported on four poles.

And I remember the man who started talking about his father-in-law. He'd had a shed, much cluttered, and was in it every day, until he died. 'It was an Aladdin's cave, that shed,' he told me. Not only had his father-in-law collected and stored all manner of things over many years, but he had tagged and labelled each and every item he'd acquired. So a stack of corrugated iron would bear the inscription 'Mrs Worthington's roof, lifted 3 December 1961'. He'd noticed this, for the first time, when they were clearing out the shed and disposing of the contents after the funeral. The labels had amazed him. He wished he'd found out more and done it sooner. But he hadn't. 'It's a pity,' he said thoughtfully. 'It's like a story we were never told.'

At least we have these stories you are about to read. They speak for themselves, and for everyone else who has a shed tale to tell.

Jonathan

A shed is where dreams get made

By rights he should be dead. Fifteen years ago, a sleepy stroll at 4 a.m. took Jonathan seven metres off a balcony. It wasn't exactly the comfort stop he'd planned. And since he hadn't really been awake when it happened, he was greatly puzzled to come to on very solid ground with a neck that wasn't working as it should. So with one hand holding his head upright and the other on the steering wheel, he drove himself to hospital. When they looked at the vertebrae in his neck, they found not one but two hangman's fractures. Either should have been fatal, but neither was.

Now Jonathan spends two hours a day in traction, listening to music and looking out to sea in the shed he designed and built by himself after the accident. He lives and works in his shed and is fighting to stay there. In spite of the fact that they gave him a building permit and charge residential rates, the local council wants to move him on. Jonathan won't budge. He loves his shed.

Where it is, what it is, the fact that other people have lived and worked there for a hundred and fifty years – as he does now, making furniture and boats. He's built a boat for himself ('It's even got a shed. There's a workbench in the fo'c's'le with a vice and tools.') and now he does the same for others. He works on the simple, elegant wooden craft for two to three hours a day or until he gets too sore.

'I come from a long line of woodworkers, so I've got to have a shed. You get more bang for your buck with a shed. I mean, this place owes me five grand and I can get on with what I want to do rather than fill my life with trappings. I'm a shed person from way back. Shed people are people who do things. And doing things involves dreams, but you can't have dreams without a place to make them. You can't have dreams without sheds. A shed is where dreams get made. I need a place to make my dreams.'

Steve

If I didn't have a shed,
I'd die

Hidden away in an industrial estate, Steve's battered old shed doesn't catch the eye. If anything, it looks more likely to catch the bulldozer. But the rusty iron exterior simply means the occupier is preoccupied. Not with how the shed looks, but with what he can do inside it.

'If I didn't have a shed, I'd die' – it's as simple as that as far as Steve's concerned. 'I'm a man with a great love of sheds,' Steve says. 'I'm supposed to be retired, but if a man sat on his arse all day he would die, like so many others. But I've got too much to do. I don't feel like dying.'

Even so, age has forced a few compromises. Steve's started using a little scooter to get round the yard 'when m'legs are too tired. It's years of bloody hard work – they've stuffed m'knees. The joints are worn out.'

There's not much else that is, though, as a shed tour reveals. In one small room Steve's got an engraving business, for cups, trophies, plates and name tags. Further along, there's the garage where he keeps his large and impressive Kawasaki Kumagutzer Mk 1. He's done 16,000 km on this three-wheeled hybrid, with Toyota engine and Triumph diff. That could change, of course. Steve's got so many modifications planned he doesn't think he'll ever finish.

At the far end of the shed is what Steve's called 'The Solo Mothers' Discount Room' – even though his mates seem to be its chief beneficiaries. This is his brewing division, well stocked with liqueurs and spirits. 'There's always one or two in on Friday nights for a tasting.' He thinks he's produced 'an acceptable product' because 'a few of the old sheilas come round and they're pretty fastidious about what they drink'. There's a pause, and a grin. 'I'm happy to give them a sample. You never know, I could get lucky. Even a blind chook picks up the odd bit of corn.'

Not today, though.

Today, he's trying to unravel the mystery of the outdoor furniture. He made it before, years ago, after spotting some pieces salvaged from a fire. But now he can't work out the patterns at all. Sitting at the bench in his workshop, Steve scratches his head. 'It's got me beat. But I'll get there. It won't beat me. It might all end up in the tip . . . but it won't beat me.'

Mike
I love it out here

He can't remember what it was called, but the tune has stuck in Mike's mind ever since he heard it more than forty years ago. It was just a jingle, the theme for a show, but that melody unchained something that's never gone away. It's the reason he's set up his own shed station, and if he could track down a tape of the tune he'd play it every day to launch the breakfast show.

Mike grew up on a dairy farm down south, in Riverton. As a nine-year-old, he would flop bleary-eyed out of bed at 4 a.m. to help with the milking. He's never forgotten the old cowshed, its chaos and clatter, or the way the early morning misery would turn to wonder when he'd switch the radio on just before 6, in time for the 4ZA theme. Sure enough, it put a spell on him, so much so that, years later when he was working in Australia, Mike would once again get up at 4 a.m. just to hear that magic music.

Of course, back on the farm, it wasn't only the breakfast show that fired his imagination. By the time he was twelve, late at night when everyone else was asleep, he'd creep back to the cowshed to listen to the world chatting away on shortwave.

Eventually, Mike got involved with ham radio himself and for years that was it. Until the day he found out you could set up an ultra-low-powered station without a licence, and before you could say 'Golden Oldie', 98.8 Alpine FM was on air. It's probably one of the smallest stations in New Zealand, with a 300 milliwatt transmitter, one advertiser and no obvious format. There's an ecletic mix of music from sampler and promotional CDs. And Mike just wanders out when the mood strikes and has a chat.

'I love it out here, introducing things and welcoming people. But if someone comes round and asks if they can have a go, I say "Yeah! Rip into it!"

Since Mike went on air, he's built an audience within the station's 5 km radius. But out in his 'shack' he's trying to reach someone else as well – a little boy in a cowshed who dreams of a theme at 6 o'clock.

Nick

If there's no mess, you haven't done anything

There's a problem at Nick's place and it involves the shed. There are extensions planned, you see, at the back of the house. Trouble is, the extensions are designed to go precisely where the shed already is. Nick thought he had a solution – relocation to a brand new carport and shed at the front of the section. But now the time has come to switch sheds, he can't do it, can't leave his 'historic place'. The family are rather less reverent. They call it the D.O.S. (the dirty old shed). Which it is, of course. That's why there's a problem.

'It's no good, a clean new shed. It's not the same,' Nick insists. 'You need a mess. If there's no mess, you haven't done anything.' He compares sheds with chefs. 'The best ones are always the messiest. They don't care what they do with the gear. It's what they produce that counts.' Nick's certainly produced plenty in the D.O.S. At about 9 o'clock at night, after the children's storytime, he's off 'to make something from nothing, to create things'. Like a mantelpiece or glory box, piano stool or wheelbarrow. 'That was tough. There's not many right angles.' He's made whimsical toys, cupboards, a vanity, cheeseboards using old parquet flooring and a magnificent kauri briefcase.

Nick's always been a 'fiddler'. As a boy he kept a knife in his pocket to whittle wood. And access to a shed saw the floodgates reopen. 'The pleasure is in the innovation. You get old timber that's done time on a tree, been milled and used a part of a house. But when it's finished, it doesn't go to the tip or get burnt. It has a new lease of life . . . It's a continuation . . . that old wood keeps its place.'

Also in place these days is Nick's son, Henry, eagerly creating his own adventurous wooden artefacts, using the 'wonderful' wood and brass tools Nick inherited from his grandfather.

Nick's delighted someone else appreciates the D.O.S., with its carpet of shavings and friendly wetas on the workbench he rescued from the dump. 'I couldn't get this environment anywhere else in the section,' he says, as the cicadas shrill in the trees. 'I can't bear to shift.'

So, for now, the extensions are on hold. In the words of the whittler, 'The old shed prevails.'

John
Cut it twice and it's still too short

Perfectionists would understand the compulsion. Another 'woody' could see why it takes 130 hours – three weeks in the shed – to make one of these mini-mansions. Calling them dolls' houses is like saying the Taj Mahal's a bach. Neither description captures the builder's passion for perfection.

In John's case, the same goes for the furniture. He'll spend twelve hours working on each tiny table or bed, longer on something like a high chair because its spindly framework is tricky to assemble. So is the tea trolley he's currently making. It will have movable castors, of course, a full set of little wooden plates and cups and its own miniature oak cake stand, like 'one my mother used to have'.

He admits there's more detail than the most demanding Barbie would require. And he doesn't know why he's 'so fastidious. It's just the nature of the true woody, I suppose.' He concedes that he's always been somewhat contrary. 'There's only two sorts of people,' says John, 'the lunatic fringe and the zombies!' Very definitely one of the former, he says he quit being a sun-worshipper when he found nudists 'have no conversation'.

During World War Two, John drove an ambulance in China and on the Burma Road, then worked building boats 'that weren't poured out of a bottle'. The job honed his skills and also provided the same frustrations he experiences now. 'Cut it twice and it's still too short' is an adage he hasn't forgotten.

Today, John's houses, like those old boats, are beautiful and functional. There are no fronts 'because they break and get in the way'. He has watched children play and designs the buildings so they can move dolls around easily and get maximum fun out of all that intricate furniture. John has an album of the pieces he's made. He says he looks at the photos and sometimes even he 'can't tell if the furniture's full-size or miniature'.

Unhappily, he's lately hit a snag. 'I got pneumonia last year. I stayed out in my ruddy shed day after day, finishing something, and I got too cold.' It's a bone of contention, he says, because now 'I'm not allowed out after tea'. Except, he says quietly, when his wife has to go to an evening meeting . . .

Alan
A shed can never be big enough

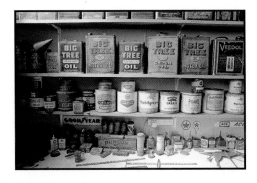

If Alan's wife hadn't wanted some bottles, he wouldn't have his shed or the collection in it. But she did want some, to brighten up the house. And quite by chance the first boxful Alan acquired included one old oil bottle. Just one, but that was enough. His curiosity was aroused, 'and I wondered what else was out there. Before too long the disease just snuck up on me. It's a way of life now.'

A way of life that's seen him build a vast new shed to house his growing array of 'petromobilia'.

'When I built this shed I thought, "Great it's huge." But when I moved things in, I wished it was an extra four metres long. A shed can never be big enough.'

It's easy to see why. Currently, Alan has eighteen vintage petrol pumps, assorted signs, many faded boxes stamped Plume, Sky Chief, Big Tree or Voco and hundreds of oil cans, many pre-1920 when brands like Germ, Zerolene, Veedol, Speedwell and Sternol (makes engines purr like pussies) were the market leaders.

Some of his pumps also date back to the period when cars were an unproven novelty. The earliest is a 1910 Gilbert and Barker kerbside, which was wheeled out to waiting motors. Alan's also restoring a 1912 Red Century bowser to go with his 1918 Avery Hardle, the 1922 Australian Hawk and his spectacular 'visibles' – so called because their glass cylinders 'let you see what you were getting'.

Many of these pumps were hand-cranked, like those used by Power Chief in the careless days when their trademark was a warrior's head with full moko.

A later prize is an electrically operated Palometer. It was produced by Pallo Engineering of Wellington, once proud makers of the only range of pumps designed and built in New Zealand.

For Alan, 'every piece tells a story', and that is their fascination.

What began with one bottle is now a significant archive. Like much in sheds, these relics of our motoring century are easily overlooked. But who knows, if one of the pumps was draped in a condom, it might even make it into Te Papa.

Joe

Everything from a horseshoe nail to an anchor

The faded sign on the back wall is one of the few clues that this is a trailblazer's shed. But that's what Joe was back in the 1950s. He used to cut wood – until one Saturday morning when a saw nearly severed his finger. Eventually the finger healed, after a fashion, but not before Joe had to quit his job.

'The insurance policy paid £6 a week. There was £3 to pay off the house and £3 to feed Mum and two kids. Things were getting hard so I thought I'd sell what I had and live off that.'

But at £15 his woodcutting gear found no takers.

Then someone asked if they could use it for a day for £5.

'I thought, gee, this is a good racket. I've still got it and I've got £5 for it. That's how I started. People would ring and want a drill on Saturday and I'd go to the hardware store and buy it, then hire it out. All the stuff was brand new, but I never bought anything till I got a request.'

Joe thinks his hire service may have been the first in New Zealand, 'although there was one other in Christchurch that may have started earlier'.

Over the years, he says he's hired 'everything from a horseshoe nail to an anchor'. And sometimes even family possessions. His wife recalls the Christmas Joe hired her cake mixer, and the year all the pots and pans went out. But her most vivid memory is the cot.

'We had a brand new baby and Joe hired out our cot. I had to turn the sofa towards the wall to put baby in!'

Happily, there's been an up side. The kids were always paid if anything of theirs was hired. His daughter had a tent that went out summer after summer. 'She made a fortune out of that,' chuckles Joe. His son did well out of the Saw Gulliver in the shed, using it to earn pocket money sharpening saws. And anything Joe couldn't hire he'd convert, like the old bed end that's become a bar in the lounge.

A heart attack two years ago has slowed him down. But the shed's still open and Joe's still doing what he's always done. 'I've always been a great believer in sitting and thinking how to make a shilling.'

So far, it's worked.

Trevor
Old posts and corrugated iron

Gourds aren't exactly common in New Zealand. Related to the cucurbits (pumpkins and the like), they grow on vines and produce little white flowers that are pollinated by moths at night. Maori voyagers brought hue (gourd) seeds with them, using the vegetable as a food source. They also used shells as containers and to make musical instruments.

Trevor's always 'enjoyed growing different things' so when some seeds came his way from Australia, he planted them in a glasshouse. 'I didn't know about the moths,' he says. Mercifully, at least one got in and a single fruit was pollinated. A year later, he planted the seeds outside, not really expecting anything to happen 'and got seventy plants'. That's how it all began.

Sixteen years later, he plants in October and harvests in April. The gourds go onto the shelves of his drying shed for six months, till the outer skin's 'all rough and mouldy. Then I scrape that off with some hi-tech tools – a kitchen knife and a Goldilocks – and get down to the very hard shell.'

It's the shell that has seen gourds used, for centuries, as food and water containers, drums and maracas. Trevor's not making those, but he is 'supplying people who are reviving traditional Maori instruments; they need specific shapes so they can make particular instruments.'

More generally though, he carves 'semi-abstract patterns', his own designs, into the shells, then paints and seals them. 'Most would be opened at some stage,' he says, 'so people could use them as containers. They're sold as decorative pieces, but they can be used.'

Trevor's shed incorporates a gallery, built the same way as the drying room, with 'old posts and corrugated iron. I enjoy building a shed like that. It's a challenge to build out of what you've got.'

As one of the few people working with gourds in New Zealand, he's often visited by collectors. And his gourds 'have gone to every country in the world'. But it's still 'a labour of love,' Trevor says. 'You're never going to be a millionaire working with gourds. It's very time-consuming. People who work with gourds just enjoy it, love it. I have a whole lot of fun. Selling is a bonus.'

Dick

I can be here all day

Last year, Dick was in hospital, in urgent need of surgery. After the operation his wife, Louisa, asked how he was feeling. Dick's answer was emphatic: 'I wish I was back in the shed.'

No, she wasn't surprised, Louisa says. 'I've even thought about putting his bed out there.'

Well, they have been together fifty years – Dick and his shed – thanks to a large slice of luck early on. 'When I built the shed in 1946, I fell through the roof,' recalls Dick. 'I thought I'd killed myself . . . but I grabbed a runner and that saved me.'

Originally the shed was just for his garden tools and general paraphernalia. 'Then it became my second home. I can be here all day. I love the shed. You can do anything here, practise any hobby you like. If you see a market innovation of any sort, you think, "Crikey, I wonder if I can make one of those?" Well, you get your head together and give it a go . . . I'm eighty-five, but I don't feel anywhere near that, because I keep myself active.'

And Dick's not the only one who benefits. The shed, he says, 'affords me the opportunity to help people'. He's a keen golfer, the oldest member of his club ('with three holes in one'), and actively involved in the children's coaching programme. Years ago he cut down a set of golf clubs for a five-year-old, and people have been asking him to do it ever since. He buys old clubs, shortens and refurbishes them, then sells them for what he originally paid. 'The kids love them.' His other occupation is making paua buttons which he 'gives away to anyone who wants them'. He's built his own cutting tool to produce the circular shapes. As to the danger from the dust, he just says, 'If the paua doesn't get me the booze might.'

Dick reckons he can also do 'anything you want' in the shed because he's got 'a bit of everything' in it. 'People don't understand loving junk. But I'm a hoarder. You never know when something's going to come up that you want.'

Richard

A bloke's lost if he hasn't got his workshop

Hoarding is a tradition in these parts. 'I've been like this all m'life,' says Richard. 'I like this sort of thing around me. Sometimes, I stand in the middle of it and just gaze . . . it makes me feel secure.'

His massive '55 by 33 foot' shed is crammed with things he's come across . . . 'things jokers were going to throw into the tip' until he decided 'to hang on to it'. He's determined to keep most of his 'old stuff', although he plans to sell the 1971 LC GTR Torana. A Holden buff, he's got a stack of engines and a 1955 FJ ute, stowed behind him, underneath the two hang-gliders on the wall. 'I'm still restoring them,' he explains, adding that one frame and motor are 'all done up'.

The ute is also 'part way through restoration', like the 1956 FJ Holden four-door behind the scrap-metal bin. Richard is also itching to finish his 1928 Erskine. 'I love that old car. I'm keener to get that one done than anything.'

But work is needed on the house. So Richard is rebuilding a tandem trailer in a barter deal with a friend. It's got a telescopic draw-bar 'so he can carry eight metres and balance the load', and a host of other modifications. 'When it's finished it'll be the ultimate,' he says. 'To buy it, you'd spend megabucks.'

Ten years ago, back injuries forced Richard out of work and out of town. He brought 'about twelve tons of gear' with him. Sadly, another injury and an illness that's left him on a 'semi-critical' waiting list for fourteen months mean he can't handle heavy work now. 'I've got it all up in my brain, but I can't do it. I get really uptight sometimes . . .'

The fact that there's 'no room in the shed to work' doesn't help. Richard's currently working outside, using an old farm trailer as a bench. 'It's a pain, but I've got a Skyline garage that I'll put up really soon, I hope, as a workshop.'

He'll need it, with tractors, trucks and a field hospital generating system awaiting work. 'I've got to limit m'self a bit,' he says. 'I'm running out of time.' But he knows where he'll spend whatever time he's got. 'The shed's somewhere to live. It's my workshop, my whole hobby. Everything is in the shed. Let's face it, a bloke's lost if he hasn't got his workshop.'

Dave
Dad was a shed addict, so am I

A UK holiday in 1985 gave Dave his first glimpse of the spectacular Countach. 'Nothing else even looked like it,' he remembers. 'It was such an outrageous shape.' Even then, there were replicas on the market. 'The Poms had taken moulds off a real one – they reckoned copyright had expired.' He shrugs. 'I just wanted one . . .'

So Dave came home with a replica, but 'it was a disaster of a shape. Really badly made.' Determined to get a 'faithful reproduction' he used the kit to make new moulds and then a plug. Twelve months later, he finally began the car he really wanted.

Others wanted it too when they saw it, and Dave decided to make more. 'I got a race-car designer to work on the chassis and suspension. The Poms had these horrible box sections that made it hit things.' But now? 'It handles like a Porsche.'

A safe one at that. 'One car has just had a big ding,' says Dave. 'It hit a bank at 160 k. The impact took the boot off the front but the rest was fine. The doors still opened.'

In 1995, Japanese drivers in the Targo Rally saw Dave's car and 'Lambo-fever hit Japan'. Dave switched from making kits to fully built-up cars, using a turbo-charged Nissan 3-litre V6. The space-frame chassis is shed-made, alongside the kevlar and fibreglass body shell, doors, bumpers and hood. Tricky components, like the hinges for the vertically opening doors, have been designed here too. 'I've had to do the same work as the Lamb designers did originally,' says Dave.

And more. 'One guy wanted electric windows, which weren't in the original. That was a nightmare, but we finally solved it.' Now someone wants manual windows.

Dave's tackled tougher problems, like getting the suspension angles right. Normally, this involves much expensive equipment, which Dave doesn't have. So he hangs a weight from a rod and uses that. Last time the angles were checked on a laser machine, 'nothing needed changing'.

Nor is it likely to. The business has 'grown out of a love of doing this sort of thing. Dad was a shed addict, so am I. But Jackie [Dave's wife] said I had to tell you – behind every good man in his shed is a wife pushing him along.'

Rob

When I'm home, this is where I want to be

When he introduces himself, Rob likes to add the initials SCF after his name. 'That's my qualification,' he says mischieviously. 'School Certificate Failed.' But what he missed at school, he found at sea – and then some. 'Ships and boats, they're all I know,' he says. 'Boats run in the family. My father and grandfather were at sea or involved with ships.' Rob himself was sixteen when he went to sea in 1951 as a deck boy. His first ship was a coastal collier sailing between Greymouth and Auckland. Later he worked on the old Cook Strait scows, and then ashore as a harbourmaster and a wharfie.

Rob still sails but these days it's just for fun. The boat's rather different too. He built it himself in his back yard. It took eight years to finish the two-masted timber schooner which features, amongst other things, sails hand-sewn by Rob and '5600 rivets. My wife's counted them.' There's one piece of gear that's more visible and certainly more treasured. 'Dad made the wheel,' says Rob. 'I may have to sell the boat some time, but I don't want to sell Dad's wheel.'

That's not all he's reluctant to lose. 'I've got my father's and grandfather's tools in the shed,' Rob says. 'When I grab hold of something Dad had, it's a nice feeling.'

Most afternoons he'll 'go and play boats', but the mornings belong to the shed. There's always something to do, marine repairs or a bit of tinkering with the truck. 'My wife's father bought it in 1938. It's never been out of the family.' And neither have some of the other prizes Rob's got in here. 'Dad built both large models,' he says, 'and I've got one from Grandad as well.' One of his father's models is on the bench, the other behind Rob on the truck's running board. Maintaining the tradition, Rob makes models too, and also restores them for other people.

'A shed's a man's domain,' he says. 'The only thing Val's got in here is the clothes basket and pegs. I like my time out, as we do. And I love sheds. I could be on the boat, but when I'm home, this is where I want to be.'

Doug

It's beautiful equipment

Multi-storeyed sheds aren't common and tend to go up, not down. This, however, is the exception. It's a bunker really, going six metres – twenty feet – underground, with room for a 'basement' and mezzanine floor beneath Doug's chair.

These hidden depths are a legacy of the time when the building was a borough pumping station. Doug was the engineer here, tending the two pumps that still survive, six metres below his lawn. Changes to the water supply made them redundant and gave Doug the chance to buy the property when he retired in 1987. These days, he's using the old station to 'pump' something that does have waves but isn't water.

Doug's a ham radio fan, and a keen one too, provided the equipment's 'all valve and no transistors'. Integrated circuits, looking like 'little black beetles on their backs, waving their legs in the air', do not feature here.

Much of his gear, therefore, is old and rare, including his 'famous' Collins transmitter. 'It's beautiful equipment,' he says. The 1955 Collins was gifted to Doug three years ago 'on the understanding that it would be gifted on when I'm finished with it'. There's also an ancient Collier & Beale transmitter he intends to restore. 'They're all gone now,' says Doug. 'All the good things go.' During World War Two, he says, Collier & Beale made superb 'silent' receivers which coastal raiders couldn't detect.

Most days, Doug spends about four hours in the shed, listening to the Concert Programme or talking on air. There's a group he communicates with regularly: 'sometimes six people, sometimes two. They're all in the North Island, but I'm able to talk worldwide. I value the gang I'm mixed up with', partly because 'the whole world's indifferent to each other now. In the street where I grew up, you knew everyone and everyone looked after each other. Today, they don't even know you're there.'

But the gang does. 'We'll talk about "shoes and ships and sealing wax, and cabbages and kings . . ." the weather, or how the country's being run. Years ago, you wouldn't dare say you didn't like the government. It's like broadcast radio,' says Doug, 'everything's more open now.'

As it should be, in an 'underground' shed.

Geoff

Dad's workshop — impossible jobs done immediately

Geoff has a challenge he likes to issue to those who visit his vast and much cluttered shed. In fact, it's the clutter that makes his challenge irresistible.

There's all the gear from his speedway days, when Geoff raced a home-built Mustang. Plus the various components of current restoration projects and the ones Geoff reckons he'll get round to – someday. As well as the tools and materials involved in several 'top secret inventions'. (Of these, Geoff offers no details beyond the deeply cryptic 'If you think you know all the answers then you haven't asked all the questions.') There's a wall hung with a dusty array of spare parts for his ageing harvester. And another stacked roof-high with boxes full of fiddly things. Add a workbench completely buried in 'stuff'; several sizeable machine tools he built himself (including a guillotine to cut the sheet metal for his race car); the very large indoor silo next to the teetering piles of tyres and tubes, and the impression of total confusion is complete. And considerable. This is, after all, a shed built in the early 1940s by Geoff's dad to house threshing mills and the like.

So there's ample room for chaos to expand. And every reason for visitors to accept Geoff's invitation to test him with an apparently impossible task. 'You name it', says Geoff, 'pick a bolt or screw, nut, rivet, engine part and I bet it's in my hand within a minute.' Something suitably exotic is named and Geoff goes off for a rummage. In the boxes or along the bench beneath the sign 'Dad's Workshop – Impossible Jobs Done Immediately'. If it's not there he heads for the big doors where the old Ford slogans are still visible. 'Fastest on Race Day' says one, 'Fantastic Over Rough Dirt' is another. Some doubter once scrawled 'Fix Or Repair Daily', but that's been scrubbed out.

Not so Geoff's memory. He meets the challenge. In fact, he always beats the clock. And finds what he's looking for. Including intangibles like the satisfaction that comes from tinkering with his veteran trucks and tractors. Or fixing his neighbours' machinery. He's even found romance here. In less crowded days the shed was the venue for some great parties. On one memorable night a young lady 'got left behind at the end. And she's been here ever since' – as his wife.

Adam

It all began, as these things do, with just one shed

Adam reckons he's spent years in the shed. There've been plenty of times when he's gone down to the shed at night, got involved in some project or other and walked out into the light of a new day. A young niece of his was convinced Adam didn't like his wife because he was always going outside. Conversely, on one of the rare occasions in the last thirty years he did stay inside to watch telly, Adam fiddled so much he got very clear instructions to 'get down to the workshop'.

It all began, as these things do, with just one shed. Soon it wasn't big enough. So Adam added on. Then built another shed. And another. Then some more. All without permits. And all with whatever tin and timber came to hand. He's straightened and hammered so many old nails he's now got arthritis in his shoulders, 'and that's slowed me down a bit'.

But Adam has no doubt that the treasure within his many sheds was worth the effort. 'All machinery is man-made,' he says emphatically. 'Except John Deeres – they come direct!'

Especially the old two-cylinder models. Because they offer a rare acoustic treat, as Adam well knows. 'All tractors make a noise. But those old John Deeres make a sound!'

It's a sort of measured, unmuffled explosion which has earned the old-timers the nickname 'Poppin' Johnnies'. And Adam's got 'em by the shedful. Along with hailers and crawlers and harvesters and ploughs. No wonder he says he couldn't survive without sheds. They've served a passion that, perhaps, was meant to be. 'I always say 1941 was the best year ever for my parents,' he explains. 'It was the year they bought a John Deere tractor and the year they had me.'

Lester

It's got to look right, if it didn't I wouldn't bother

When your great-grandfather worked on the first trams in town, and your grandfather was a motorman, and your dad turned the family air-raid shelter into a shed, there's a certain inevitability about where your preferences will lead. Mind you, in a sense, Lester's also following in his own footsteps. As a boy, he spent hours happily engrossed making models, till adult pressures arrived. 'I didn't do much then, what with all the things you have to do . . . kids, marriage and so on.'

His interest was rekindled by a model tram in a shop window. 'I thought I could probably have a crack at that.' Now, the goal is to have one of each type of tram, and the cable cars too. 'At this stage, I think I'll be about ninety when I'm finished.'

Lester spends 350 hours of his spare time making trams like the Bob Tail or Sydney Bogey. 'I'm not technically minded,' he says. 'I'm more interested in character.' So his shops, offices and houses are also accurate models of real buildings. 'I take photos, knock on doors and ask, "May I measure your house?" I measure old trams too, because there are no good plans.

It's got to look right, if it didn't, I wouldn't bother.'

Because 'I've got off my bum to make contact with old tram workers', the shed's got its share of old tickets, punches and money bags, plus a cable car bell-pull and seat. Lester's largest prize is an entire cable car front, now a dividing wall. The shed door 'is ex-tram, too. With a match striker on the inside for wax matches.'

The display's becoming popular. 'Kids can make the cable car run. They think that's Christmas.' Lester's surprised that 'when couples come, the women always ask more questions'. But not surprised that 'old-timers just open up. It's a trip back to the past for them.'

All told, this shed's a far cry from his dad's basement lair. 'There was a flex running through the floor. When Mum wanted him up, she'd switch the power off.' There are no such drastic measures now. 'I'm certainly not a tram widow,' says Lester's wife. And Lester says the theory that a shed is somewhere 'to get away from the missus doesn't apply to me'.

More than just the trams, it would seem, are happily on track.

Brian

I get withdrawal symptoms if I'm away

There wouldn't be many sheds with their own pneumatic hammer. But there's one in Brian's shed. It weighs a tidy 13 tons (certified by an unsolicited MOT check) and originally belonged in the railway workshops. Brian bought it when they closed and the hammer was sold as scrap. Better still, the vendors 'estimated it weighed a mere six tons'. So Brian definitely got more than he bargained for. In more ways than one, because the first time he tested it, the hammer head came crashing down so hard on the anvil that his wife rushed over from the house, deeply worried 'because all the crockery was jumping about on the shelves!'

Nor has that been the only complaint. 'My wife says we don't get away for holidays,' Brian admits. 'But I get withdrawal symptoms if I'm away . . . working with steel, and the riveting, just gets hold of you.' Not surprising, when your riveter weighs over a ton. With gear like that, it's just as well 'when I built the shed, in '65, I put a travelling crane in as well. I couldn't be without it, it's my handyman.'

He surely needs one. This hangar-sized space is really a factory, a reassembly line for Brian's cherished road locomotives, traction engines and log haulers. Some he displays, including a 1902 6-h.p. Burrell Traction Engine and a 1927 Aveling & Porter 4-h.p. (multiply by nine for the petrol equivalent) beast, plus a 1904 8-h.p. three-speed John Fowler road locomotive.

By his own admission, Brian's a perfectionist: 'Everything's got to be just right.' Especially now, as he rebuilds the 1904 Burrell his grandfather once owned. The amazing thing is that, single-handed, Brian makes whatever's too rusted or damaged to restore. He's already built a new plate-steel firebox, new barrel, side plates and back plate for the Burrell. 'It's fascinating,' says Brian, 'the way things were done in the old days. One has to appreciate the hard work our forebears put into making this sort of equipment.' And there's also 'something about steam. An engine can be as dead as a doornail, but a bit of TLC and it comes to life. All a steam engine needs are the three main elements – fire, wind, and water. That still fascinates me.'

Greg

It gives me shelter . . .
and it gives me atmosphere

The first winter Greg was here, it never stopped raining. He put his workbench in the only dry place he could find, screened off another area with a canvas fly, and moved in. 'It was as cold as buggery. Water kept pouring in . . . That was the best year of my life. I was on fire, working fourteen hours a day . . . Trusting my senses, seeing how it felt to be free and wild, in a totally new town where I didn't know anybody.'

Nor did he intend to buy a 19th-century brickworks that had lain abandoned for forty years. Greg came here in search of scrap timber he could turn into furniture. But then the owners offered to sell, and that was that. Even though the floors were 'three feet deep in rubble. It took ten days just digging it out.' And another two years of hard labour before he had a tolerable place in which to live and work.

Greg's furniture-making began just helping a tutor, 'making breadboards and alphabets. Then I made four chairs, a table and a rocking chair. A guy came in and put $500 on the table. I'd never seen so much money in my life. I was away. There's nothing like cash to motivate you . . .'

But it's not the only incentive. Many of his large pieces now experiment with forms inspired by bone carving. And Greg enjoys the 'timeless' quality of simple things like cottage chairs. 'They came out of workshops like this and slowly evolved year by year. I enjoy carrying on that tradition.'

A diving accident seven years ago nearly made that impossible. It crushed his fifth vertebra, and even now 'I've still only got half-strength in my upper body. But I was so fit when I did it; y'know, the wild man, working here – that's why I survived.' To build his dressers and tables and rockers. And savour the joys of his super-sized shed. 'It gives me shelter, it allows me to make furniture and it gives me atmosphere, the environment I want. I've got an old bath outside and I light a fire underneath and sit out under the stars in the steaming hot water and I think "I might do it in stucco one day."'

Drew

Some nights we just come down and have a look around

Any adage addict knows Necessity is the Mother of Invention. In this case, it was also the Mother of Investment. Mind you, that wasn't the original plan.

The saga started fourteen years ago with three brothers in search of space to work on their cars. So Drew, Steve and Jay – all hot-rodders to the marrow – rented part of a downtown shed, with plenty of room to cut and chop and bore and grind. Until the dark day five years ago when the landlord decided to sell. 'We had to buy it,' recalls Drew, 'we had to. We couldn't afford to move out!'

If there was any doubt then, there's none now. Not since they've taken walls out, moved engines in, installed extra benches, created more space. The shed is here to stay. 'It will be a permanent part of my life,' says Drew. 'We could never move. There's too much gear. You'd never shift it.'

Arrangements here are very democratic. All the bills are split three ways.

All the tools are shared. And VT (vehicle therapy) is available for those in need – like the brothers' sister's boyfriend. 'He used to be into Valiants and crap like that. Then he started going out with my sister. So we steered him off those and got him into cars.'

There are plenty here. A 1956 Ford Mainline Pick-up, a 1927 Model T Roadster, a 1932 Ford Coupe (soon to be joined by a 1934 model), a 1921 Dodge T Bucket and a very tasty, jet black 1955 Chev. Little wonder the shed is much used and much prized.

'Some nights we just come down and have a look around,' Drew says. 'Y'know, we don't do nothin'. . . just stand around and have a yap.'

Somehow, I can't see these guys ever going to a Gold Coast timeshare evening.

Robert

This is my sanctum sanctorum

Precision is a significant part of Robert's life. He's a horologist – a watchmaker – or, more exactly, 'a watchmaker's watchmaker'. Robert enjoys doing, is driven to do, the jobs others don't attempt. He's repaired two- and three-hundred-year-old timepieces declared beyond redemption by overseas firms. He's fixed long-stopped church, barracks, mission and museum clocks in the Islands. Once, working on a mission clock that hadn't ticked for sixteen years, he was surprised to see a crowd gathering. 'People walked seven miles to see the white man who worked and got dirty. Until then, the only whites they'd seen were administrators.'

But Robert's mastered more than time. 'I used to race motorbikes. It cost too much to fix them, so I started doing it myself. That's how I learnt to use tools.' Since then, he's acquired a good number, including a power hacksaw, sheet-metal bender, argon arc welder and bandsaw, and used them to produce his own plane, a Jodel. It took him thirteen years to build, and it flew in 1994.

Wartime experience servicing altimeters and gyros means he's still asked to test or repair air-speed indicators, barographs and ancient instruments that 'modern avionics can't fix'. But it's clocks, watches and jewellery that the shed principally serves. Robert still fashions the sterling silver sleeper earrings he began making years ago. 'When I started, they took fourteen minutes to make. Now, I finish a pair in two minutes, eight seconds.' In 1981, Robert sent a pair of 14-carat sleepers to Princess Diana as a wedding present.

The sleepers – and clocks – require specialist equipment, much of which is created here. Involute, cycloidal and hypoidal movements all need special tools. Glass-making is 'a self-taught skill', and Robert's built his own bevelling machine and more besides. Work arrives here from many parts and Robert micro-engineers it all. 'This is my sanctum sanctorum. If you have a passion for your work and it gives a challenge, you're not satisfied until that challenge is resolved. You get frustrated with a clock that's 200 years old. You make a part for it, like a wheel, then find that no cutter you can buy will shape the teeth. So you make a machine to make the cutters to make the teeth . . . It's like playing the piano. If you stick at it, and if you're any good, it will eventually come right.'

Bill

Any day not spent in the shed is a very bad day

The Wright Brothers would approve. So would Richard Pearse. Because all his life, ever since he can remember, Bill's been teased by a mysterious compulsion to design and build his own aeroplane. He doesn't know why, it's just always been there.

At sixteen, he marched into a bookshop and – sight unseen – ordered 'a book on aircraft design'. It was the standard textbook on the subject but it wasn't much help. Bill remembers 'the wall-to-wall mathematics . . . it might as well have been Hebrew'. So the tome gathered dust. As did the dream.

Until the morning years later, when Bill suddenly woke and thought 'Right! I'm going to build an aeroplane. It was as quick as that. I just knew I had to do it before the neurons got burnt off.'

He went back to his textbook. To understand it, he taught himself algebra – on the farm, in the paddock, while he was keeping an eye on the grain drier. Eventually, he mastered the maths – and the manufacture. In the shed, of course.

Because any day not spent in the shed is a very bad day. It's a disease, he admits, incurable and terminal. And if he can't satisfy 'the irresistible urge to make something', grouchiness sets in. His shed's not a place, it's an addiction. Alternatives like golf ('chasing little balls with knobbly sticks') don't rate.

'At least after I've wasted a day in the shed I've got something to look at, something that wasn't there before.'

Like his magnificent planes: the (currently) wingless super sleek Snark 1 single-seater and the equally tasty Snark Mark 2, a high boom two-seater with pusher propeller. This is the Snark Bill hopes will go into on-demand production. Which would keep the shed humming. And Bill too. He likes to quote Chuck Yeager, who once said, 'The secret of successful retirement is always to have three years work ahead of you.' Not a bad goal for a man who's done the right stuff, all by himself in the shed.

George

It's a nice area to have a quiet cup of tea

The eels are the big thing. There's a goodly number to be found, which is what brought George back here twenty-two years ago. He was brought up in the area by an uncle. Then, as now, people had their own 'drains', ditches for the eels to swim into and be caught. A drain in the right place ensures a good catch. George's best is 2500 in one night.

He started eeling young. 'When the old people were playing cards, we'd be down there having a go.'

He still is, but these days the drain is his. Not that it's a monopoly.

'You help others dig drains,' says George, 'and let them use your drain. There're about fifty regulars every year. When the eels are running, the bush telegraph gets going and out they come. And the people who've dug drains have got a lot of relations. There's always someone here.'

And something to do. The flax in the shed, for instance, brought by a friend, will need to be shredded to hang the eels. 'I've never got around to making mats or baskets,' says George. 'I suppose I should have.'

But for now, it's all eeling. Catching, smoking, maintaining the drains. When the eels aren't running, George gets the flounder nets out of his shed. Add to all that the stacks of concrete blocks from a toilet George demolished to use for an orchard wall, plus manure and the like, and it's little wonder George refuses to part with his rusty and immobile old Datsun – 'It's handy to keep things in' – or that his shed is bigger than the house.

'I'm a shed man definitely,' George declares. 'Of an evening, it's a nice area to have a quiet cup of tea, watch what's going on, or listen to the sea. It tells you when it's in a bad mood. During the winter the seals are out, waiting for fish.' George surveys his kingdom.

'It's a great view. This is the beauty of it. Just to see people at night, torching away after the eels.' He pauses. 'I thought about going over to the West Coast' . . . then grins . . . 'just for a visit.'

Peter

They're the secret of youth, sheds

He's a self-confessed 'picker-up of bits' whose friends call him 'weka'. Doubly apt, since Peter's always loved the outdoors and growing up in London, wanted to go farming. 'But my family were all academics. They said farming had no future.' Happily, Peter prevailed and went off to an English farm. 'A cousin of Ed Hillary's worked there. And after the Everest climb Hillary turned up . . . he said he was a boundary rider on a bee farm. I was so enthralled by his descriptions of the mountains, and New Zealand, that I applied to come here.'

Eventually, he got a job in Bluff as a shepherd. Within a year, he'd learnt to ride horses, shoot pigs, cull deer and live in a whare. He also discovered collecting. 'There was so much old stuff there. Like the vintage cars that were put on blocks during the war and stayed there.'

Peter's first car was an old Model A, which he sold when he got married, to buy a sewing machine. Nevertheless, his weka-ish instincts were roused and Peter started accumulating – old pews, hand pumps, windmills, 19th-century milk separators, all manner of bric-a-brac. And cars. Lots of cars.

Peter presently has two Jowetts awaiting restoration, plus two Model T's – a completed 1920 truck and the 1913 Tourabout he's rebuilding. 'I like the word "challenge". And the challenge of restoring a Model T is as big as any.'

To get much needed parts, Peter 'turned urban archaeologist and dug up the old Ford garage tip where all the old stuff was dumped. My wife suggested we form a company – "Dumplings".' Now the bits he salvaged are safely in the shed, along with his rare Blackstone stationary engine and much else a weka would prize. What he hasn't got, this 'bush mechanic' will make.

Peter admires the DIY tradition. 'They're very versatile people, New Zealanders. In the UK, everyone's a perfectionist. They only make screws or whatever. But versatility's the name of the game today. If you're not versatile, you're history.'

Looking back, Peter's glad he's 'learnt a lot through necessity' and can apply it in his shed. 'Everyone needs time out. My time out is out in the shed. If you've not got a hobby before you retire, what do you do with yourself ? They're the secret of youth, sheds.'

John
I can let myself go

Music was a big part of John's boyhood. The photography, ham radio, computer and writing came later.

'Dad was out playing every night,' John recalls. 'With the Orphans Orchestra Club . . . a whole range of bands. They used to have orchestra practice in the lounge. I remember it as clear as anything.'

That was back in the 1920s, and what Dad did then in the lounge, John does now on the computer. It's the perfect outlet for a frustrated musician. 'I've tried to arrange Mozart,' he says, 'but it gets so monotonous. Jazz is more fun.' John's arranged hundreds of pieces out in the shed: Bach, Chopin, Debussy, Dixie, Handel and Hot Club. His orchestra's more hi-tech than the old Orphans, with his instruments all synthesised so that 'if it sounds awful I can try different instruments, different tempos'.

He's able to do the same sort of creative tinkering with his photographs. John installed a dark room and processing room when he extended and bricked the old fibrolite shed in 1960. Since then, he's made his own scanner so he can digitise pictures. 'All the photos go on the computer and I can alter them, add graphics, whatever. It's so interesting to put them on screen and try various effects.'

One effect he's not keen on is atmospheric interference. 'It's hopeless,' he says. 'Radio reception used to go in cycles – eleven years good, eleven years bad. That used to correspond with the plant growth cycle for trees and crops. The theory was you got a bumper crop every eleven years.' But since the 1980s, things have got out of kilter. 'Something's spoiled communications,' he says. 'El Niño or whatever, so you just talk to whoever you can contact.'

Add 'the stories of my childhood' John's now writing and storing on his beloved Amiga – sometimes with photos – and it's easy to see why he spends so much time in the shed. 'I can let myself go and be as rude as I like. And I never have to think "What am I going to do now?" There's always something.' He usually breaks about 8 p.m. for a nap, then comes back at midnight 'to see what's going on in Europe. I talk to people there who've just got out of bed till about two, then go to bed myself.'

Not a bad day for a man who's eighty years old.

Burns

Cobwebs are absolutely essential

Cobwebs, as far as Burns is concerned, are absolutely essential. 'I caught some bugger last year – a cleanliness fanatic – trying to clean the cobwebs up. Hell, it took twenty years to get them like that.' And he's not about to see them go. There's an abundance of cobwebs in Burns' sheds. He has two, one to paint in – 'that's where I work' – and the other, this one, for sculpture. 'This is my favourite,' he says. 'It's where it all began.'

Art has always been a magnet. 'My mother painted, she was a wonderful encourager.' As was Colin Wheeler, who taught him at school. But his father's ill-health meant that 'when I came up to farming age, I left school and ran the farm'. Somewhat eccentrically, he concedes. 'I saw everything in terms of creativity. If I found a leaking trough, I'd plant a willow tree rather than fix it. That doesn't make for a very good cockie.'

But he always kept going, inhibited by the view that art was 'quite poofy. I had this fear of appearing effeminate. It took a long time to grow out of that.' Eventually, the 'consuming passion for sculpting' won and the farm shed became a studio. Once described by his mum as 'an inveterate collector of unconsidered trifles', Burns used some of them to build the six machines he has in the shed, including 'the Bufferonium. I use it to polish sculptures. It's got a beautiful action. I think we're much the poorer for losing the ingenuity to build and make and fix things . . . It's an important part of our make-up, the ability to create necessities in the shed. But that's going. Nothing gets fixed now, it's replaced. And we're losing the buzz you get out of creating and doing things.'

Today, Burns paints full time, mainly because 'it's more viable'. But he still spends time here. 'Solitude's very important. The most priceless thing we've got is thinking. There's a whole generation today who can't handle silence . . . They haven't learnt the incredible satisfaction of knowing yourself, on your own.'

That's a satisfaction Burns has got from his shed. 'It's your world. And with any luck no bastard can get in. It's a haven – like going back to some sort of womb. This is my patch and it's like an aura, a boundary around me.'

Colin

There's something about old sheds

Colin's a man with a family of sheds. An irregular array is scattered down the garden path that leads to the largest of all, the one with a turntable so he can get his bikes in and out easily. It wasn't meant to be this way. 'When I came here,' says Colin, 'I intended to knock the old sheds down. But I never got round to it. Instead, I built another three or four.'

The population explosion started when 'the garage was crowded with bikes. Getting in and out of the car was like a circus act.' So sheds began popping up. 'Not exactly Fletcher Challenge', but they did the job. A caravan, originally used 'for School Cert study' now houses a 1960 305 cc Honda Dream – and the cat. There's a shed for the Kawasaki Voyager Colin's bought; a shed for his welder and compressors; wooden sheds; kitset sheds. The motorbikes have driven this expansion. Colin got his first bike when he was sixteen, in 1946, and his latest – a 1200 cc Suzuki Bandit – last Christmas. Having 'been through BSAs' and 'gone off English rubbish', Colin's focus now is 'vintage Japanese'.

He's got a 1973 Kawasaki Triple ready for restoration and three 1974 354 Honda CBs as well. Others on the list include a Yamaha step-through, a Hercules push-bike with power-pack, a little Italian Moto Becano and a rare 1979 Honda CBX6. Colin's just finished a Z50 'kid's fun bike' and a Honda CB 440.4 trail bike rebuilt 'from a heap. I took every nut and bolt to pieces on that one.'

Today, Colin's enjoying the benefit of 'twenty years of working weeks, weekends, nights and Saturday nights'. He and his wife have clocked up 11,000 miles, touring on the Voyager. And when he's not on the road, he's likely to be in one or other of his sheds. 'I can't be idle,' he says. 'There's something about being down here. It's about feeling worthwhile.' For Colin, 'sheds pertain to people who like to be industrious. People who fix their neighbours' go-karts, or fix their neighbours' lawn-mowers.'

He puts a bike on the turntable to back it under cover. 'There's something about old sheds,' says Colin. 'I'm buggered if I know what it is . . .'

Geoff

To have a shed — it's such a buzz

No matter where he is, wild beach, lost valley or mountain stream, Geoff has always got his shed. It travels with him and his wife and two boys wherever they go. And they go wherever they like.

Geoff's always been 'a traveller at heart' and for the past ten years he's been a traveller in fact, roaming the country in his housetruck. Three years ago, there was an addition to the family — a 2.8-litre Daihatsu diesel double-cab. It was 'a rusted-out heap' but Geoff fixed it up, then built his steel-frame, ply-clad, four by two-metre shed. It bolts to the deck of the 'support truck'. On the road 'we live in the housetruck and Lisa [Geoff's wife] drives the support truck. Then, if we park up, I take the shed off, put it on legs and we drive around in the double-cab. It's like a car for us. Damn fine!'

The porta-shed has its own generator. In the old days it took 'two hours to set the workshop up before I even got started. Now, I can be miles from civilisation, walk out, pull the cord on the generator and I've got a shed like everybody else.

It's great.'

Geoff's a carver, working with jade, carnelian (a bright orange/red agate), dark argalite, beach pebbles and petrified wood. Some of the jade he buys, 'but all the other materials come for free, by fossicking for them'. The jade is used for jewellery, 'fish hooks, abstract koru spirals, small wearable stuff'. Geoff also enjoys 'sculptural work' with the other stones, carving high-relief forms on a surface and experimenting with paua inlays on white beach pebbles. 'I spend about six hours a day in here when I'm busy. It's like a job. It keeps us alive.' Add the washing machine, welding gear and tools and it become a shed for all reasons — including Geoff's peace of mind.

'Every man's got to have a shed. And being a carver, it's almost like a temple. The place you go to be creative, experience that creative part. And you get lost in that — you transcend the world. It's almost meditative . . . a very nice space. I do things I couldn't do anywhere else. To have a shed — it's such a buzz.'

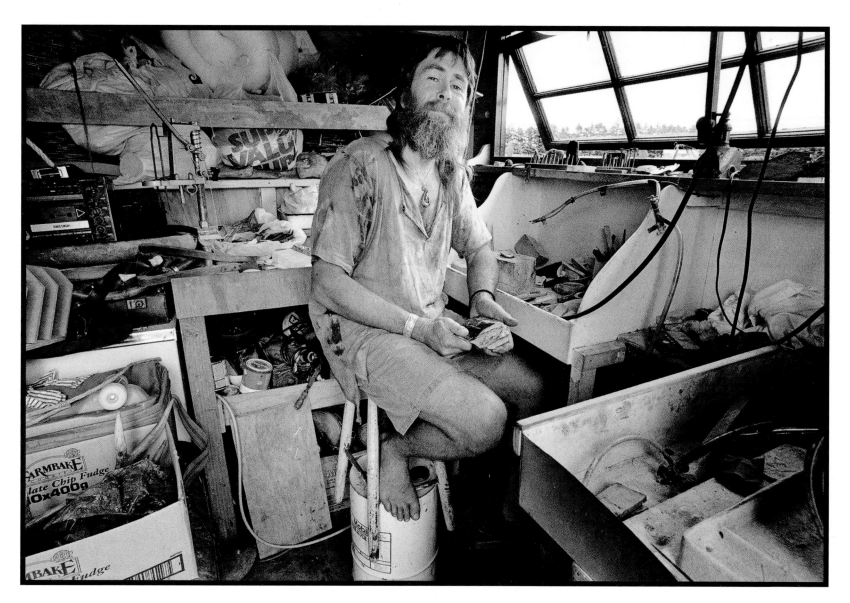

Snow

You name it, I make it

Two months before he was due to retire after ten years of working as a carpenter for the NZED, Snow was 'finishing whacking on a roof. I'd been crouched down for four hours doing these big, long rafters. They'd been cut green and were all bent and twisted. So you had to clamp and bolt them as you went. Well, I stuck it out to the finish, thought "Thank God", stood up and blacked out. I don't know what happened after that. If I'd landed on my head it might've been all right. As it was, I became a paraplegic in two seconds flat.'

The fall occured fifteen years ago, soon after another terrible tragedy. 'My wife died and I had the accident all in one hit,' says Snow. 'It was very hard to keep going. But if you put your mind to it you can do it. You've got to keep on living, no matter what happens.'

At the time of his fall, Snow had been building his own retirement shed. 'I just didn't quite get it finished before I got wiped out,' he says. Originally planned as a garage and workshop, the 30 foot long by 20 foot wide building is devoted entirely to woodwork. 'I make rocking chairs, kitchen chairs, coffee tables for friends. You name it, I make it – anything in the furniture line.'

Snow reckons he completes something 'once a week', ranging from 2 metre dining tables to form seats with turned legs. He also repairs any pieces friends bring round. 'I don't charge anything. I do everything for nothing.'

With a full range of tools, and a duplicating lathe, thicknesser, routers, band saw and press drill, he can tackle most jobs, although he admits, 'If I'm handling something pretty big I've got to make something to hold it for me.' Or get somebody. Snow says he's lucky he's got 'lots and lots of friends. It can sometimes be a full-time job making cups of tea and baking cakes for them.'

A former climber, he admits, 'I really miss my mountains.' And that he'd 'be lost without the shed. There's something about wood. It's really nice. And there's always a sense of achievement when someone really appreciates what you've done for them.

'It's most essential, a workshop. All men – even women – need hobbies for their old age. Something you can get your mind into, keep yourself busy. Forget your miseries, that's the main thing.'

James

You have to do something; if you do nothing, you die

Ganagobie sounds like the sort of medical condition it's best not to catch. Happily, it's not an ailment but a place, the French coastal town where James grew up. Translated, Ganagobie means 'big fish' or 'flying fish'.

Easy to see why, when James builds an aeroplane, it's a Ganagobie too. He creates his own designs, this prototype being the second off the drawing board. The tiny spruce and plywood single-seater, which he's called the Ganagobie Mousebird, is definitely one for the pilot with a mouse-budget. James has spent $6,000 so far and estimates another $6,000 will see it in the air. That total includes approximately $3,000 to buy and convert a car engine as the powerplant. He's no newcomer to aviation, having spent seventeen years working for the French light aircraft company, Jodel, and another four with a firm that produced motor-gliders. It was in France that James designed his first aircraft, the Bushbird. One of these two-seaters is on display at the Experimental Aircraft Association Museum in Oshkosh.

In 1969, a job offer lured James to Australia. Then, unexpectedly, 'the lucky country' proved to be anything but. 'I lost my job,' James recalls. 'You get to fifty-five and they don't want you any more. So I had to prove to myself I could still do something. I felt the Australians had put me down, you see. It was a matter of pride.'

If pride was the spur, New Zealand was the place to build his aeroplane.

'The rules are easier here. You have an experimental category so people can fly their own design.' James says safety is not compromised, there's just a minimum of bureaucratic interference. This is why the microlight industry is booming. The shed situation's different as well. In Europe, says James, he'd likely be building in a shed or workshop owned by an Association that rents space to members. 'You drive maybe fifty kilometres to get there.'

Here he's leased a shed 30 seconds from home to build his Mousebird. 'This is a challenge for me. You have to do something; if you do nothing, you die. I am here practically full time. Except for Monday – I've got a girlfriend now, so that's my day off.'

Peter

I get carried away here

Sculpture is the driving force here. At least on the ground floor. Upstairs, where the view is better, Peter paints. When he built the shed ten years ago, it was going to be where he would turn a hobby into an occupation. Excited by his 'tragic firings' and general 'pottering', the Yorkshireman from 'Freddy Trueman territory' thought, 'I can make a go of this.'

Except that things haven't exactly gone to plan. 'It's not paying the wages,' Peter concedes. 'There are no grants coming this way. It's all me own funds. I only get pulled back by the ones I manage to finish.' And that has proved rather difficult for a perfectionist who loves to experiment.

There's a kiln here, of course, and plenty of pots. Including one bearing the likeness of Captain Cook. 'See the big Yorkshire nose,' says Peter. 'There was a local lad who done well.' He also works in Oamaru stone and bronze and he's just found a great big piece of marble that's 'going to be a whale's tail'.

The trouble is 'I go off things so quickly and move on to something else.

Like, with the marble, I've flagged everything else away.' So pieces like his lovely wax mould of a curled tuatara (there's one of the floor) sit on a shelf in the shed, waiting to be cast. Peter has spent years on his tuatara series, even inventing a process to spray hot wax on a core. 'I'm doing it the old fashioned way – Leonardo's way, Michaelangelo's way.'

One day, the curled tuatara will go into the foundry, one day he'll finish off the other bronzes he's cast but which don't quite meet his standards, even though they look fine to an outsider's eye.

'I know they'll sell if I want them to. But I'm not marketing it very well . . . It's too enjoyable, actually. I get carried away here; I could keep going for ever.' He acknowledges that if his wife Mary wasn't working, he couldn't chase his mysteries. 'There are secrets I have to find out. I know how to do it. I'm just stretching it out all the time. Once I'm into it, it's hard to pull back. I just have to pay the bills though, things like that . . . '

Alasdair

It's occurred to Alasdair that this could be *the* 21st-century shed. It's definitely his 21st-century shed. And he means to enjoy it.

'I put up with a sub-standard shed. And all the time, little dreams were taking shape. By the time I was ready to build, I knew exactly what I wanted.' Alasdair had his plans 'finessed by an architect', spent twelve months and several thousand dollars on the planning process, and twenty-one years after he first imagined it, the shed was up. 'Nice and clean and bright', just as he intended. 'I love that. I can come home from work, fling my tie off and start on something. I'm not naturally a tidy person, I just can't bear the things that go with untidiness.'

His abhorrence of mess and enthusiasm for sheds are well known. 'One day,' says his daughter, 'he'll go missing for a fortnight and we'll go out and find him decomposing on the floor.' Which won't help the tidiness. Fortunately, there are happier things to contemplate.

'I still find it a bit unbelievable. Sometimes I just come out and look around.'

That is, of course, when he's not working on his autos, or taking one of them for a spin. Alasdair's restored a 1925 Chevrolet Tourer, a 1926 International Truck, a 1915 Buick Roadster and a 1942 Jeep, 'arguably the world's first successful four-wheel drive.' Each vehicle has its own bay, complete with shelves for parts. 'If it's not there, I haven't got it.'

There is one exception to this precise arrangement – a 1914 Hupmobile Tourer. 'I inherited the project from my father,' Alasdair explains. 'He died before Christmas. His one regret, facing death, was that he was never going to ride in it. After all the work he'd done. I started thinking, "If I could get it painted and put the body on, I could take him for a ride." A friend, a spraypainter, helped. I told him it was urgent because Dad was very ill. We got the car back. And he drove it. After the ride, his bags were packed. He was ready to go, and he died six days later. That's something I did that no one else could . . . So the Hupmobile's now part of the family. It's nice having the car, knowing he drove in it . . .'

Kay
I get bored stiff without a shed

When he's not making models or musical instruments, Kay likes to invent things. Like his robot with moving hands and arms controlled by an ingenious system of strings and small electric motors. He started the project for fun but now the possibilities intrigue him.

'No one's thought of this, but I reckon we could produce artificial muscle. I got the idea from the robot. Sinews are like ropes, so you could use a continuous string or wire that shortens when electricity's applied. Two volts and the string would contract, say, enough to pick up a cup. With four volts it would contract more, to pick up something heavier. The potential's infinite.'

That may not be apparent to the uninventive, but for Kay artificial muscle is an irresistible challenge. Now that he's thought of it, he has to see if it can be done. And he's convinced, along the way, some other 'shed person' will help him do it.

Kay's a great believer in the energy and creativity of shed people, and in the special character of sheds. 'You need the clutter of a shed. It's absolutely essential for inventing. Something lying around just triggers an idea and then you've got a solution.'

For years, he's made models. The latest is an elaborate, radio-controlled Roman galleon, with its intricate working catapult, that's still unfinished. But Kay decided he 'wanted something better to make', which led him to make musical instruments.

Five years later, he's crafted 65 cellos, dulcimers, double basses, violins and harps. He's presently repairing an 1815 harp. 'It's amazing. There's thousands of levers, self-compensating bearings. All this twenty years before the pushbike, fifty years before the car.'

Producing quality instruments is still intricate work. Kay's designed and made some twenty specialist tools for the job. 'There's one tiny plane, it took a week to make, and you only use it for five minutes on a cello. But when I get it out I feel like the bloke who won Lotto and got his ride-on mower. It's just beautiful to use.'

Later this year, Kay's going to Switzerland for a holiday. That's a worry. 'There's no shed. I've been there once and I got withdrawal symptoms within hours. I get bored stiff without a shed.'

David
This is where I keep life's treasures

David loves working with wood. 'It's kind, beautiful and it has a nice feel. You never get that with metal.' He should know, because he's the only person in the country able to repair the adjustable (metal) riddles for header harvesters. Decrepit riddles arrive here from all over New Zealand to be refurbished beneath the immobile face of the old Dunedin woollen mills clock. ('If you start it, the weight of the hands makes it run backwards.')

When there are no riddles to fix, he's produced the odd bit of additional metalwork, such as the oversize tree-bearing barrow and home-made electric mulcher which grace the estates. But wood comes first. In fact, David believes it actually saved his life. 'I was very, very ill years ago. The Presbyterian minister who was here at the time was trying to get me interested in something other than being a dead duck. So he gave me this old lathe, a home-made affair, and that was the start. It was a sheer fluke but it took my mind off all my other problems.'

His largest achievement since then has been to build the house he and Jeanette now live in. Much of the furniture, including a very grand grandfather clock, is also his work. So are the countless wooden eggs he's made as gifts. 'They're very soothing. I had an auntie who was a teacher who used them to calm truculent children. She'd sit them down with an egg, they'd start playing with it and settle down.'

He's made much more besides, but of all his shed's output, David's proudest of the acolyte torches, which were a gift for the Christchurch Priory in England. Initially, he didn't know what an acolyte torch was, so he researched their function before designing his own version of the candle-bearing standards. The wood David used was salvaged from a local church after a fire in the steeple.

He savours the fact that there's something on the other side of the world which came from his shed. Everything here is his: the tools (some of which, like the grinder and sander, he made himself), the cobwebs and the clutter. His final words? 'This is where I keep life's treasures — apart from my wife. I expect we'll grow old gracefully together.'

Bill
Restoring, repairing, repainting

Most people don't know there once were Tigers in Timaru. And Jumbos in Auckland. Bill only found out because he'd chanced to acquire 'a few old tractors'. Their tendency to occupy large amounts of space meant 'Mum was getting crook. So I sold them and decided to collect toys instead. I thought there must be some made in New Zealand.'

Of course there were, with Fun Ho the best known, plus rarer brands like Tinky Toys, Jumbo, and one of Bill's favourites, Tiger Toys from Timaru. Extinct now, Tiger flourished in the 1950s with a range of die-cast toys. Being a farmer's son, Bill particularly admires Tiger's carefully detailed farm implements. His own collection includes a post hole digger, front end loader and roller plough. They are, as Bill says, 'beautifully made', and he believes that's largely due to the high standard set by their designer and creator, Tom Mountfort.

Bill's been collecting for sixteen years and is now the proud and happy owner of more than 500 toys. He's not big on plastic playthings like the Buddy L fire engine someone gave him. He prefers lead or die-cast models and has a few rare ones tucked away.

They include some from Peak (which briefly continued Tiger's production when that company closed), New Zealand-made versions of British Triang toys, and a couple of Fun Ho prizes, a 1930s-style tour bus and an old NZR railcar. Fun Ho began in 1930 and closed 28 years later 'when Matchbox came in', having produced 800 different models. The company's old Inglewood factory is now the National Toy Museum, and well worth a visit, says Bill.

He gets the odd visitor to his shed as well – other collectors, here to swap. Indeed, Bill will occasionally cast a duplicate of a treasure, in order to produce a replica for a fellow fan. So, what with the restoring, repairing, repainting and general tinkering, Bill's busy out here at least five hours a day. And while that may not be 'as much as I'd like', it'll do.

'A woman has a house,' Bill argues, 'and it's all regarded as her place. That's mum's domain. Well, this is my domain.'

Ross

The shed's a good place to hide

'**Running out** of work' when you're forty is not pleasant. It didn't leave Ross with many options. 'I'd made a knife once as a kid. It was either that or pottery.'

Knives won. His early efforts were 'pretty rough, but you get better every day'. Now, his top knives fetch $1,000. Ross produces 'a full line of hunting knives, with sheaths, as well as small, medium and large chef's knives, right up to the ten- and twelve-inch blades'.

These days, he says, 'some real fancy people use my knives, from politicians right through. I'm not fussy who I sell them to. They just have to come here to buy them.' One thing that has surprised Ross is that women buy 85 per cent of his knives. 'They're a woman's thing, not a man's thing, even the hunting knives.'

Entirely self-taught, Ross works with steel, brass, wood, leather and bone. What's more, 'everything I use is recycled material'. High carbon steel comes from items like circular saw blades or coil springs, 'especially HQ Holden coil springs, they're good fat ones'. He's built his own forge to flatten out scrap items. But he couldn't build the Linisher, the belt sander he needed. That was

imported and Ross had to mortgage his house to bring it in.

Happily, the shed was cheaper. 'Half of it's an old raspberry stall,' he says. 'I can remember as a kid getting ice creams and raspberries from here.' He'd driven past the now disused stall hundreds of times before he realised 'it would make a great shed'.

Unhappily, soon after he relocated it, Ross was hit by a car. The accident left him with two broken knees, a broken shoulder and other injuries. He remembers ramming the clay floors of his new shed 'on crutches, one arm in a sling, pounding them down with a bit of four-by-four in one hand'. And although the accident is still 'a pain in the legs', he's since added a gallery and other extensions. Now, 'it looks a hundred years old again'.

For Ross, the shed's 'a good place to hide, get out of trouble — or get into trouble'. Not that that seems likely, with customers clamouring. 'I can do this till I'm ninety. If I've still got my faculties and can move my fingers. It's not stressful, you see. And no two knives are the same . . . they're all different.'

Arthur

Things relating to the sheds are my life

He's got two sheds, has Arthur. One for brewing and one for brooding. Not melancholic brooding, you understand, but the pondering sort of brooding necessary to solve knotty problems.

Like how to free a salmon lure that's snagged, how to reduce the nicotine intake of the addicted, how to wash your feet if you can't bend down, how to practise arm-free fishing and how to pitch a tent in less than a minute.

Out in his brooding shed, Arthur's solved all these problems – and more. Smokers, for instance, can use his 'Cut Down', a simple little cylinder that will put a cigarette out without producing a bitter aftertaste. The hapless addict can relight later, rather than start a second ciggie. Those who fish can rescue lures with Arthur's 'Snag-Away' ('It's saved hundreds') or drop their gear into the 'Rod-Holder', which clips over a car window. 'An American shopping channel was interested in that. They'd seen a photo and rang me at 1 a.m. But they wanted guaranteed supply. Setting up a first production run would have cost me $50,000.'

Arthur knows better than most that ingenuity doesn't guarantee success.

'I've never made any money. I've been on the verge of making heaps a lot of times. I've probably been ripped off more often than not.' Still, there are compensations. 'I invent for my own use, or if people ask me. I love solving a problem. I'm like a dog with a bone. I won't give up . . . and at the end there's the satisfaction of inventing something that really works.'

The same goes for brewing. Arthur's brewing shed's been set up with care. His still is heated by an old water cylinder element, the fermenting cupboard is thermostatically controlled, his mixer is, characteristically, home-made and he is fastidious about purification. 'I couldn't afford to buy the drink I liked,' says Arthur, 'so I made it myself.' Now he's brewing fourteen different spirits, to the considerable benefit of his friends.

One way or another, Arthur's sheds are his first home. 'And things relating to the sheds are my life. I can get an idea at 11 p.m. and go out there and get engrossed. Just forget the time. People enjoy my drinks and I like to invent things there's a need for. Maybe, one day, I could start an inventors' shop . . .'

Richard

I just sit in my shed . . . muck around, make things

Dumps don't often get rave reviews. But this one does. It's been on the telly, impressed several sports stars, and attracted international praise as well. 'An American girl came in the other day,' says Richard. 'She said it was amazing. She took photos to show them what New Zealand could do. She was really rapt about it . . . said we should get a visitors' book. I might do that.'

Eight years of TLC have transformed Richard's tip. The shed behind him wasn't here when he started. Just a shipping container, for storage, that was regularly vandalised. So Richard cleaned it up and painted it. Now it's where 'our recycled bits' are sold, or bartered. 'A lot of people come in and want to swap,' he says. All the clothes that come in go to the Salvation Army 'and I donate to the marae and schools for galas. We always tidy something up.'

The same goes for the container which now sports a cheerful array of salvaged signs. And poetic contributions from Richard.

One of these, which begins 'Dumpdy Doo, Dumpdy Day, Sorry people, it's time to pay' relates to dumping fees. They may vex some visitors but they were a boon for Richard. 'When I first came here, we had to bring in our own water,' he explains. 'But one of the customers complained about our conditions when the charges came in. So the council brought the water on. And gave us a nice new office.' Proceeds from recyclable sales pay for coffee, sugar, milk and toilet paper. The Pink Panther 'just turned up', like the electric frying pan that was dumped recently. A quick check showed all it needed to make it work was a new cord. 'So we use it now,' says Richard. 'It's like brand new.'

Windfalls like that are a nice bonus when you're on the job six days a week. But Richard loves his work and has plans to 'decorate the little shed and make it like home'.

A man who has 'always had a liking for sheds', Richard says he'll often go into his own, at home: 'I just sit in my shed . . . muck around, make things.

'My little boy had a wheelbarrow with no bucket to put things in. So I used an old aluminium fry pan lid – rivetted it on. And he's still got it. Won't part with it, because it's something I made.'

Jock I pull everything to bits

He was lucky not to be captured in Greece, but Jock got out on the last ship to Egypt. In Cairo, he'd haunt the silversmiths and antique shops. Even at school he'd been a collector, although then it was bottle tops and marbles.

The army frowned on souvenir hunting, so Jock dug a hole under his 'good' kitbag, keeping a double for inspections. A quick switch in 1945 and an 'approved' kitbag came home, then got lost, but three fortunately months later Jock found it.

He's found much since. Several shedfuls in fact. He bought his first shed for £25. It was an old school, no longer needed and up for tender. Jock 'dismantled it in sections and brought it here'. He's built others since, each crammed with a fantastic confusion of strange and wonderful things, acquired even though 'the biggest wage I ever got was £3,000.' Jock collects 'anything at all from a needle to a haystack. I've got something from every decade of the 20th century and most of the 19th.'

Jock likes to understand his treasures. 'I pull everything to bits . . . if it's not working, I'll fix it or keep the parts and do it later. If there's nothing wrong, I still pull it to bits to see how it works . . . I like to know the principle.'

Somewhere in a shed, carefully wrapped in cloth, is every piece of a 1906 Darroch. 'The bridge down the road was being sandblasted,' says Jock. 'I thought if I got the chassis down there, I'd get it done cheap.' That was twenty years ago. 'When I pulled it to bits I put all the details down in a notebook. Every nut and bolt, the order I did it, is in the notebook. I'll put it back together one day.'

This tendency to dismantle inspired the sign 'If it ain't broke, don't fix it.' The family's message hasn't worked. Take the (very heavy) lathe Jock recently wanted to move. He thought he could shift it himself, up a ladder, by hooking it onto his endless chain. Now, this is despite two hip replacements and clear instructions to stay away from ladders. So he climbed his ladder. And fell.

But Jock says two broken fingers won't put him off. 'I'd need to live to 300 to do everything I want to do here.'

I hope he makes it.

Pete

It's great to be by yourself — in your own little world

One for the pundits, this. A shed to inspire earnest discourse in learned journals. Is it avant or retro, neo or post? How does it stand in the vernacular tradition? How does it stand, full stop?

Don't ask Pete. He's the first to admit a good sneeze would blow it away. Then again, it only took a day to build and the result is a shed that's perfect for his particular brand of occupational therapy.

Pete, you see, has the kind of job not many would relish. Long hours, shift work, high stress and aggro are all part of the equation. Pete gets to deal with tragic situations and ugly ones as well. He's had to use force and he's been on the receiving end too. A hard, harsh occupation means Pete needs something special to download the tension he brings home.

He's found that in the exquisite delicacy of bonsai. It's a safety valve he discovered by accident when his efforts to landscape the section were sabotaged by lack of space and the unhappy tendency of neighbourhood dogs to dig up whatever he'd managed to squeeze in.

So he cut his losses and downsized. Pete says that's the best decision he's made. The science and art of bonsai are now a consuming passion and his shed is 'a home away from home. If I'm not at work, I'm down the back shed. It's my own little world down here. You get sick and tired of crowds and people, so it's great to be by yourself – no phones, no people – in your own little world'.

Pete spends hours on end in his shed, propagating and tending his miniatures. He locates each tiny tree in a specially created landscape, enhancing the effect with wires to shape branches so they appear bent by prevailing winds or otherwise sculpted by nature

These days, he's concentrating on natives – beech, rimu, totara, southern rata – using cuttings from parks and mountain areas. The ones he likes he gives away, to friends or to the school fair, or else he adds them to his own micro-forest.

So while his wondrous trees are small, the benefits emerging from Pete's sub-retro-neo-minimalist-stress-relief shed are enormous.

Ivan

The shed's my kitchen. It's . . . where
I can achieve something

When something hasn't worked for eighty or ninety years, it's great 'to bring it back to life'. That's what Ivan savours. 'I love doing it. And I get a lot of pleasure out of saving a piece of history for posterity. Some of these things would not be in existence if not for people like me.'

He used to run his own garage and, since he retired, Ivan's just kept on fixing cars and motorbikes. Especially motorbikes. Ivan's been 'mad keen' on them 'all my life'. He got his first bike when he was twelve. There were 'no road restrictions then, and the main road was still shingle. When I came back after the war, I rode around on an unregistered bike every day.'

He had a 1926 350 cc AJS then and he's still got one now. Plus a 1905 Vindec Special, a 1910 Matchless, five Nortons – including one from 1909 – two 4-cylinder Ariels, a Russian Planeta and a rather exotic, fully enclosed 1934 Royal Enfield.

But his earliest bike is 'so old it's got no name'. Moped-like, it was made in 1900 and has a pedal-start engine. Ivan's just finished making a new crankcase for the mystery machine, using the old one as a mould. The shed's well equipped for restoration projects. Ivan's kept the boring plant from his garage, 'so I can do my own reboring'. There's a complete MiG Welder, a power hacksaw, Mill drill and a 1-ton Cardiff lathe. 'I bought it from my brother-in-law. It's beautiful.'

Throw in a diesel heater salvaged from a bus and it's the perfect place to preserve his piece of the past. 'Some of these bikes have been literally dragged out of the ground,' says Ivan. 'The shed's my kitchen. It's the place where I can achieve something.' And he's adamant it's not a retreat. 'A lot of men have sheds to get away from their wives. That's not the case here. My wife's been a marvel. I couldn't get rid of much without her knowing it. She'd miss it . . . she would!'

Doug and Gerald

The lure is strong

Red River threshing mills are rare indeed. There's only one in New Zealand, stored here in the Vintage Machinery Club's most sizeable shed. Club members like Doug and Gerald work to preserve vintage equipment such as the mill, much of it from farms. 'We're pretty tractor-minded,' says Gerald. He remembers, as a boy, seeing one particular tractor at a show. 'I couldn't believe it,' he says. 'It was red and cream and I thought, I'm going to get one of those one day.' And he did, and it's here. Gerald enjoys the solitude here. 'It's a good place to hide, get away from the work and the doom and gloom on television. At times,' he says, 'my wife politely suggests I should bring my sleeping bag here. But she knows I'm not getting up to mischief.' On the contrary, he believes he's doing something important. 'This thing can't talk,' he says, pointing to a tractor. 'It's people who talk. The stories my father told me were about people with real personalities. They couldn't survive otherwise. It was slave labour, really – hard, hard work.'

Doug agrees. A former Club President, he retired from farming in 1995, making sure he had a shed under the new house. 'It cost me a lot of money, more than the house,' he says. Part of his 1800 square feet of shed space is 'The Ratbags' Nest'. 'Most nights, young jokers come in with a problem. We muck around with that then relax in the Nest, covered in grease and oil and dirt.' Doug's got eight tractors. Gerald, who sold his farm in 1990, has kept two. Both say they'd be 'absolutely lost' without sheds. 'It'd be diabolical,' says Doug. For Gerald, 'the shed's a land substitute. You can work at your own pace, in your own way.'

'I just like doing useless things,' Doug says. 'Like working on the machinery. Women call them boys' toys. Maybe. A lot reckon it's because we had no toys, or bugger-all toys, when we were kids. I don't know if that's anything to do with it.' Whatever the reason, the lure is strong. Gerald remembers a time he went to buy a tractor. 'The guy said, "Don't come before dinner." Well, I got there just before and he was in tears. Selling that tractor, he was saying goodbye to forty years of his working life. It was quite emotional.'

Lindsey

Sheds are very important – they're evocative of past ages

Come the revolution, when the shedmen rise up to ransack the coffers of Creative New Zealand, demanding recognition and respect, this man will be there.

Unless he's in his shed. He loves sheds, does Lindsey. 'I've always had a shed.' There are two at home – one built in a day, the other rescued from the dump. Down the road, the oldest building in the settlement is his main working shed. Then there's the old red shed at the harbour. Last year he heard whispers of plans to pull it down. So he worked there too, to prevent demolition.

'Sheds are very important – they're evocative of past ages. People don't build sheds any more. Not the ones that sag a bit, with bumpy dirt floors. Now they build those horrible unaesthetic council-approved things.' Lindsey will tolerate no such travesties. A shed's got to be old. And preferably red. Like the one he rescued. 'Every woe and worry I had in the world – when I walked in the door, I'd lose them. I'd get the smell of the linseed oil, the cedar, the pine and I'd lose it. I'd never want to come out again.'

Lindsey's theory is that males generally are starting to feel redundant; but not in a shed. 'You don't have to be politically correct in a shed. You can curse and swear 'cos it's just you and this thing, which can fight back so you have to respect it. It's like a relationship with something inanimate.'

Lindsey lived in his shed for a time, only coming home at weekends. He knows what drives him. 'It's to do with creativity. Things have to look right, do right, smell right. For me, if I'm not making things and putting a bit of me into it, I'd be in the loony bin. It's forced on me . . . I have to continue.' Which he is, crafting elegant little sailing skiffs modelled on the oysterboats of his Celtic ancestors. He's made fifteen so far, calls them 'my babies' and admits 'it hurts to see them go'. They'll never make him wealthy. 'I make about $1.50 an hour when it comes down to it', but then again, it's not about money. 'I do believe there are links that lie within us which we can't understand. Mine is with the sea. I tried to move inland once. I got three miles and was homesick.'

He won't try that again. He's here to stay – by the sea, in a shed.

Geoff

A shed's more fun than a house

Seven years ago, this was going to be a hayshed. Well, that's what the original permit was for. Since then, the boat's arrived, and the family, and much more besides. Initially, Geoff's plan was to build 'a forty feet wide by sixty feet long' farm shed. Then he decided to restore the old 1936 ex-Harbour Board pilot launch: 'I thought we'd live in the shed till I could build a house.'

That hasn't happened yet. There's been too much to do in the shed. As well as work on the boat, which Geoff intends 'to rebuild on traditional lines — but with sails as well', he's also put up greenhouses to one side of the building. 'We're growing *Agave tequilana*, and we're going to make tequila from it,' he says. 'It's possibly the first tequila establishment outside Mexico. Certainly the first in New Zealand that we know of.' Getting the seed was 'a hell of a job' but there are now 2000 well-established plants.

In addition to cacti and cruising craft, Geoff likes 'building things out of heavy bits of stuff. I like using things that are thrown away that I can see beauty in. If you can be addicted to re-using things for purposes other than they were intended for, then that's what I suffer from.' He's made some 'giant' tables, a 'tallboy kind of thing' and a 'quite large, oblong hot tub that holds six people' and moves around 'with old Bren gun carrier wheels at one end and farm machinery wheels at the other.'

Geoff's also acquired an old World War Two mine that had been a pressure cylinder for a farm water supply. Attracted to its roundness and rivets, he's turned this 'really nice hunk of steel' into a stove, welding a chimney at one end and 'feeding the wood through the hole where they bolted the detonator'.

Such unorthodox comforts mean 'I'd be uncomfortable going into a house now,' says Geoff. 'If I went into a carpet-filled house, I'd feel out of place.' The shed, he says, 'is a family-friendly place. I encourage the kids to build things and use tools. With machinery and ideas you can build whatever you like. I'm still amazed what you can do with a bunch of boards. A shed's more fun than a house, better value. It's educational for the kids. At least they can do something.'

David

Understanding is more important than remembering

What started out as a six-stand, walk-through milking shed for dairy goats has become an unlikely factory, producing sophisticated, expensive, high-tech agricultural equipment. David is one of thirteen shareholders in a company that designs and builds on-farm pasteurisers. No two are the same, although all are built to exacting MAF standards. Indeed, says David, a MAF inspector has told him their PC-controlled machines are 'two years in advance of the major international players in terms of their overall design, the compactness and automation'.

Each shareholder contributes their own skills. One writes the computer software that drives the pasteurisers, another oversees 'the electronic interface'. Each machine is purpose-built for a particular client. When the design is finalised 'we clear the bench and two of us work together building the physical pasteuriser,' says David.

The venture began twelve years ago, when he wanted to pasteurise goats' milk on-site. 'There was no information, so I just asked, "How do you do it?" And Terry, the dairy farmer nextdoor said, "I know." And drew one. Classic! He's

a very clever man. And it shows the capacity of dairy farmers. They're great sources of ingenuity.'

The pasteurisers aren't cheap, costing about $100,000 each. But since they can treat beer, fruit juice, ice cream and eggs as well, demand is growing. 'We've got more work than we've ever had,' says David. In fact, he's got plans to use one to produce a single malt whiskey. There's a 25-litre still elsewhere in the shed now and, if tests with a pasteuriser work, he'll build a 1000-litre version. And if the whiskey is any good? 'I'll sell it. If not, the worst thing that can happen is I'll have barrels and barrels of it here.'

The shed is also a good place to think, particularly about education, a subject he has a very direct involvement with, since one of his children is home-taught. There's no wall in front of the desk, so David has a great view out over the estates. 'I've been known to sit in the chair for half an hour, three-quarters of an hour. I've got a very good relationship with my oak trees. It's amazing what you learn through observation. Anything that happens is an opportunity to learn from. Because understanding is more important than remembering.'

Albie

It's a real challenge

Twenty-five of the finest old stationary engines came here with Albie when he decided 'to get out of the rat race'. He loves hearing his engines 'poppin' and bangin' away' and savours 'the joy of getting them running again'. Because 'they don't make them any more', he's determined some of 'the great plodders' will remain so that 'the younger generation can get an idea what they were used for'.

These days, he concentrates on New Zealand engines. He's currently working on a Christchurch-made, 1906, 12 h.p. Anderson. 'I'm making a new carriage for it,' Albie says. When finished, it will weigh three tons and feature 'big cast iron wheels and a turntable. The timber's eight by eight . . . they used to drive everything off them.' All told, he's got twelve Kiwi engines, and others from Australia, America, England and a 10 h.p. Czech Slaviamotor that's 'the only one in New Zealand'. His largest engine is a fully restored 'twenty foot long, eight foot high, five ton, 156 h.p. English Davey Paxman'. Once used to drive a West Coast sawmill, Albie still gets it going 'now and then to keep it running.

I've got an old Bedford truck engine I use as a starter motor to turn it over.'

With 25 engines here, Albie's built a big 6 square metre shed where he keeps all the restored ones. At some stage, they'll be joined by the twelve awaiting restoration in his workshop. He also fixes stationary engines for others. One, that's displayed in the Okaina Bay Museum, had been 'rusting away on a beach for fifty years. It took two years to free it all up, six months to get the piston out of it, just soaking it in diesel.'

A vintage buff, Albie has a 1905 windmill ('they're still the cheapest way of pumping water'), a chaff cutter, grinding mill and turnip chopper displayed on his lawn. So the sheds see a lot of him. 'I don't know how I ever had time to go to work,' Albie says. 'It's a real challenge, but it's worth it once you see them going. My wife wouldn't be able to put up with me if I didn't have a shed. I'd be inside all the time, annoying her . . . No, I'm glad I've got a shed. I like getting out and playing around.'

John

It's remembrance – that's what this shed's about

You could call this the engine room. It's a bonus shed, really, additional to their own. For instance, at home, John (centre) works on his bikes and a 'wee Morris Minor' for his wife. 'Men like getting their hands dirty. So you need a shed – or a good sized garage.'

And an extra shed – this one – if you happen to belong to the Antique Firefighting Equipment Society. The Society bought the old school bus depot to have somewhere for 'all the gear that's too good to scrap'. Current restoration project is the truck behind John and fellow society members Geordie (left) and Fraser (right). It's a Fordson Thames, much prized for its unique double cab and much the worse for wear after years in the open. 'These old trucks could tell you some stories,' says John. 'Like knocking out power poles on the way to a fire, or going up to the nurses' home to pick up girlfriends. People make good use of them – love in an engine, all sorts of things.'

Such excursions aside, the old engines represent the history of the local brigade. Like John, most society members belong to the brigade. And so, on a warm summer Sunday morning, they're down at the station restoring order after a long night dealing with 'some idiot lighting fires in the rubbish bins'. Clean-ups aren't popular. Geordie remembers 'coming back from dirty plantation fires with thirty hoses to wash. It's no fun but you do it, have a beer and you're one big happy family.'

That's what they are every Sunday morning, when everyone drifts in for a yarn and a game of pool. And the station becomes a shed. 'Yeah, it does,' John happily agrees. 'It's our play hut.' With its own special traditions – like 'Sunday School'. It begins 'about 12 o'clockish' when the padre arrives to bestow his blessing. Then, when 'all sins are forgiven', the bar's open till 1.30.

Some of the 'worshippers' have been coming for more than 32 years. John hopes the Antique Firefighting Equipment Society will trigger similar loyalty. He believes 'it's a part of being in the brigade. It's good for the old guys to see the old trucks looking good and polished up. It's remembrance – that's what this shed's about.'

Len
A lot of people bring broken things to me

His own calculations suggest Len's spent close to a third of the last twenty years out in his shed. 'My wife would say I'm out here sixteen hours a day.' But he estimates it's a mere seven or eight. 'I'm one of those fortunate people whose hobby and livelihood became one,' Len says. 'I used to be a fitter and turner and enjoyed it so much it became a hobby.' One that still plays an important part in his life. 'A lot of people bring broken things to me. The pleasure I get is from helping them. I'm involved, you see. It stops you from being isolated.'

Sometimes, he'd prefer a little isolation. Particularly when 'various missionaries pop up while I'm in the shed'. As a polite way of sending a signal, he tells them a story about his father, who maintained an immaculate garden. 'Some Pentecostal soul chanced to remark, "Isn't it wonderful what the Lord can achieve!" And my father said, "You should've seen it before I gave him a hand."'

Mercifully, the majority of callers aren't after his soul, but something more basic – like a pop rivet. 'They look around the shed, with things everywhere,' says Len, 'and when I walk straight over and get it, it really surprises them. It surprises me sometimes, too.' But he's not surprised by the regular requests to use one particular piece of equipment. Len's eyes light up when he talks about his 3-ton Dean Smith and Grace 10-inch centre lathe. 'It's the Rolls Royce of machine tools,' he says emphatically. 'I couldn't be without it.' He was without it briefly, however, when he came to New Zealand from Wales. But he missed it so much he bought it back from its new owner and shipped it out here. 'I've used it constantly ever since.'

At 75, Len's adamant that 'the good thing about growing old is that you don't have to compete. You can do what you like.' Since that's what he is doing, Len sees no reason to change. 'Next time I come round I might have the pinny on and my wife will be wearing the boiler suit . . . but I hope that only happens in 200 years time!'

Harold

It's a bloke's area. I feel at home here

Mai mai (pun intended), this is surely a shed for the sportsman. And that Harold is. Every May, for instance, he and his two sons make a total commitment to duck shooting. Harold's just finished a new 'state of the art mai mai. We get the big cammo net, go in with blackened faces. If we could change the colour of the whites of our eyes, we would.'

The result of such endeavours is a shed packed to the gunwales with stuff. 'Some friends call it the cave', and the family joke is that if anyone needs to find Harold when he's within, 'they need a rope around their waist, a packed lunch and a Thermos'.

It wasn't always like this. 'We used to have good parties in the shed,' Harold recalls, 'smoking fish we caught on the boat. But not recently . . .' The rot set in when he decided to semi-reitre and 'do more fishing, duck shooting, diving . . . so-called men things'. Now the shed's chocker. There's all the gear off his boat, which he's refibreglassed and is about to refit. Plus the dive tanks, fishing rods, tents, camouflage nets, gas lights, cookers, kerosene lamps and 'spares for everything. I could be self-sufficient in here.'

The 'chaos and disarray' sometimes frustrates Harold. 'It's a bloody shambles,' he says. What puzzles him is that, when he's working as a pharmacist, he 'hates messes. I won't have a mess at all.' He suspects part of the problem is that he's 'a procrastinator – because I'm a perfectionist'. That's why 'there's millions of projects out here. The shed's full of projects I've started but not completed.'

But there are some he has finished. Harold points proudly to a gas welding set. 'You need to learn things,' he says. 'I decided a while ago to learn one new thing every year. So I went and learnt arc welding, gas welding. And it's fun. You can do things.'

In the end, clutter notwithstanding, Harold agrees with the friends who call the shed a cave. The important thing is it's his cave. 'I should've been in tool-making or lathe work or machinery, I think,' he says. 'But I can do all that in the shed. It's a bloke's area. I feel at home here.'

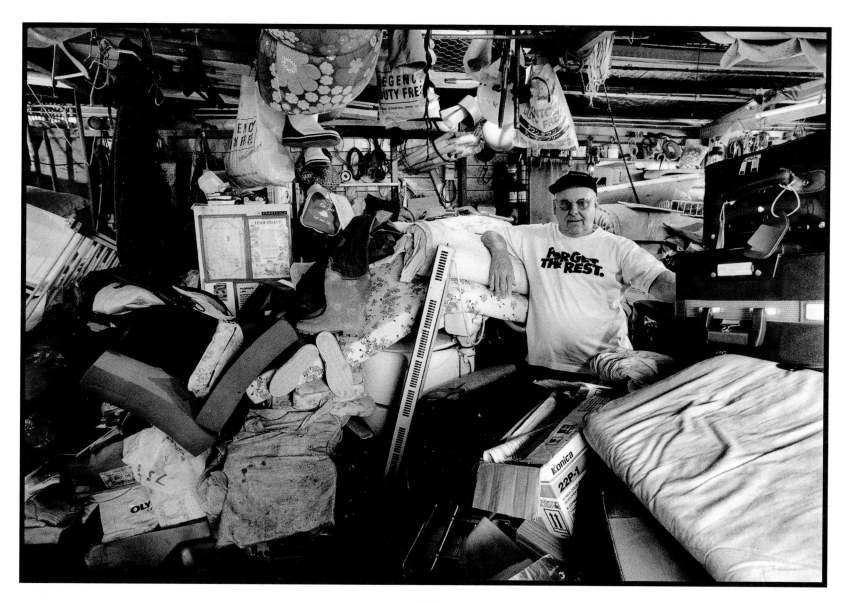

Calvin

Sheds keep things safe for the future

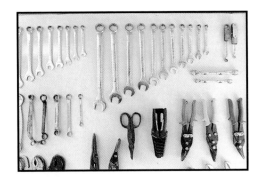

If there was an award for the nation's neatest shed, Calvin's could well take the trophy. 'I just have a dung out now and again,' he says. It must be very thorough, because if the shed is 'a hell of a mess' when he's welding a chassis, you'd never know it.

This is a well-equipped workshop, with MiG welders, a gas plant, and painting and panel-beating gear all on hand. 'I do my panel-beating the old way,' he says, 'with Dad's tools – a hammer for each job.'

Calvin's always been keen on speed. But 'when you're young you can't afford the things you want to do. When you're older and have a dollar or two, you can go and relive those things. It's your second childhood. Maybe one day I'll start bowls or join the Volunteer Fire Brigade. But ask me in fifteen years. Right now, I'd need to live to be 200 to do all the projects I've got lined up.'

All of Calvin's projects are Hot Rods. He's especially keen on Fords. 'I'm into American cars. They're more basic, not so fiddly. He's got five cars in various stages of completion, four Fords – including a rare 1934 three-window coupe – and a 1933 Willys. When finished, it'll have a Mustang engine, Zephyr diff, Triumph sway bar and Victor front suspension. His recently completed 1934 Ford Sedan Delivery is also 'made up out of bits and pieces', including an XJ6 diff, Ford 302 engine and a CV automatic gear box. 'Others say every nut, bolt and split pin has to be as old as if Henry Ford did it. I cheat,' says Calvin happily. 'My cars are all my own.' Making a chassis he calls 'a labour of love'. But the same could be said of the painstaking restoration of bodywork and meticulous standard of finish.

'I get as much enjoyment out of making them as I do out of driving them,' says Calvin. 'I like creating things – it's the challenge. My wife comes out and helps sometimes. And good mates know where to find me.

'Sheds keep things safe for the future. I don't want our heritage dumped in a paddock. I'd rather hang on to it, so even if you do nothing, it'll be in a good enough state for someone else to do something with.'

Sam

I love sitting in the shed, hour in and hour out

Walk into Sam's shed and you encounter an almost indescribable sound. Two hundred clocks, continuously ticking together, in time. A battalion of loose dentures might sound like this. Or metronomes on parade. For Sam, 'it's a noise like rain'. And it is that too, a sort of measured, metallic dripping. With it's own special benefits.

'I go out into the shed and in two seconds I can be asleep,' Sam says. 'It's very therapeutic.' Except at 12 o'clock when he wants to listen to the news 'and all the clocks start to strike'. Sometimes he hears 'a clock that didn't strike right. And by the time I've found it, the news is over.'

But if correcting time takes time, so does keeping it. Every eight days, Sam spends six and a quarter hours winding the clocks in his shed, then another hour devoted to 'the overflow'.

All told, Sam's got 430 office clocks, kitchen clocks, mantel clocks, cabinet clocks, school clocks, steeple clocks and Gothic clocks. Ninety per cent are American, the oldest an 1868 advertising clock 'with the trader's name on. They used to be all the go.' The rarest is an 1890s Fusee clock, a type that was chain-driven so it didn't go slower as it ran down.

The collection began in 1982. Sam's interest was triggered by his son, also a clock collector. 'He used to bring them to me to fix. And if it was just simple parts, it was no hardship to put them in.' Obviously, he enjoys 'preserving a bit of the past times' but can't explain why blokes become such compulsive collectors. Sam's wife, Jean, has an astute theory.

'They've probably got more time to look,' she says. Still, 'it keeps him from lifting the pot lids'.

That it does. A retired fitter, Sam's now got two sheds. The tiny one he built 52 years ago has become a workshop for repairing, restoring or building clocks of his own. That occupies six hours, the 'display shed' another four. Sam keeps a small folding table there for minor repairs.

'I spend nearly all day outside,' he says. 'I love sitting in the shed, hour in and hour out, repairing clocks.' As for sheds, 'a lot of men look on them as a place to worship'. Why? 'Well, it's just not so interesting doing other things . . . I'm an obsessed man!'

Arthur

It's gone from a mild infatuation to something bordering on insanity

Most people simply use them and toss them on the bench when the job's done. That's because tools are generally seen as a means to an end. The things you have in order to do the work. But not here. Here they are work.

Fourteen years ago Arthur's uncle left him a sack of old tools. 'I didn't want his bloody tools, so I threw the sack in the shed until one wet day I dug it out and had a look.' It was the bobbins plumbers used to use to straighten lead pipes that caught his eye. They were made of lignum vitae, a wood so heavy it won't float. Originally, he thought he'd sell the tools when he retired. But now 'I can't part with them. It's gone from a mild infatuation to something bordering on insanity.'

Arthur has over 5000 tools in his shed. There are tools for tuning organ pipes, tools whose purpose is a mystery and tools to repair the tools he collects. There's even a foot-operated umbrella maker. The oldest tool is a 1750 Lovage plane. 'Five generations have cared for that,' says Arthur. 'I wouldn't do it any

harm.' This is a man who can't abide people using screwdrivers as chisels and thinks his old foot-operated lathes, jigsaws and drills make more eco-sense than their electric counterparts.

Modernity does not appeal to Arthur. 'Today a guy hits a button, a machine gives a fart and out comes a kitchen. He gets the money but what satisfaction? There's nothing to cherish. A tradesman makes two people happy. The person who's got the thing and the tradesman who's made a good gadget.'

Skill is something Arthur prizes. It's part of the history of his tools. 'Everything I've got has a story.' He once turned down someone else's collection 'because I couldn't love them. They'd just be an asset.' He picks up a superbly crafted wooden tripod, built by the first movie cameraman on the West Coast. 'I'm not religious. But when I look at this I know that man "shall have everlasting life". Because I've got his tripod and I know he made something beautiful.'

Bruce and Warren

If we've got the gear, we'll give it a go

It's a large shed, and not in the most tropical of regions, so it can get cold in winter, especially at night – until the old potbelly stove's fired up. And it often is, says Bruce. 'We've had ten or fifteen guys round the stove, having a yarn . . . and a beer. You don't get much done then.' But they make up for that. Bruce and Warren spend hours working in the shed, and on the shed. They've concreted the floor and dug their own pit to work on their cars. They're right into cars, although Bruce concedes there was his 'blowtorch' period. 'I was off work, I'd had this op and I had to stand, I couldn't bend over. I was getting driven silly so I started restoring blowtorches. They were something I could do without bending. And they're brass, so they shine up well. They're quite decorative.'

These days, Bruce is back to his first love. He used to build and race stock cars – his was a 1937 Chev Coupe – but Warren does the driving now. Or will next speedway season, when they've finished building the Escort. They've also got a Mk 1 Zephyr that Bruce spent ten years restoring, a Farmall H vintage tractor, a 1947 Chev truck and two other Chevs that will end up as one restored car.

Both say it's a way of life, both say they've learnt a lot. 'When I started on the truck,' says Bruce, 'I didn't know how to gas weld. Six months later the truck was on the road. I'd taught myself . . .' Warren says they're both the same: they will 'try anything. If we've got the gear, we'll give it a go.' When they go on holiday 'we take the little truck. You never know, you might find something that'll come in handy for us.'

Father and son both say they could never be without a shed. They don't expect to leave this one. Nor does it ever leave them. 'You go to work,' Bruce says, 'and start pondering. You think, "How do I solve that problem?" Then you come home and you go and do it. That's what a shed is. After you ponder all day you come home and you do it.'

Henry

Nothing happens in here unless I want it to happen

A carver needs plenty of light, so the shed Henry's built is an all-plastic affair. 'It's lovely and warm in winter,' he says. 'But in summer – from 11 o'clock on – it's too hot, till late evening. I don't have time to keep it tidy, but it's what comes out that's important.'

Of that there is much. Carved figures (tekoteko), panels, moulds and castings, furniture, greenstone jewellery, bone carvings and van repairs are all done here. The van's used by local groups, including Henry's own trust. 'I don't know why I operate it – it costs more than it makes. But I have fun doing it.' The retired policeman says he's learnt plenty too – even how to make punga pots 'on a bush lathe a friend and I built'.

Given all this, it's not surprising that Henry's also discovered The First Law of Shed Volume.

'When I built it, my wife said, "Oh, that's big enough." Then the priest came down and said, "It didn't take long to fill that."' But Henry can still find room for the rimu stumps he's salvaged to make tables. 'God designed them,' he says. 'I just cut them out.' He's also experimenting with ways to cast his totara carvings in concrete, including one of a chieftain and a kiwi. 'It tells how the chief loses his children and asks his kiwi friend to find them.' Henry's view is that these tekoteko 'are the Maori version of garden gnomes'. That's why he wants to produce them in permanent materials. 'There are hundreds of stories,' says Henry. 'I want to bring them out slowly so our youngsters can be proud of who they are and what they are.'

As part of this goal, others use the shed, principally carvers working on large panels. But it is definitely Henry's space. 'I've got a need to do what I want to do, achieve what I want to achieve. The shed fulfils that need. I do everything but sleep in it. Nothing happens in here unless I want it to happen. I've just been away for a week and I left a spanner on that bench. The first thing I said when I got back was "Who took my spanner?"'

Neil
I like the satisfaction of doing it myself

The unshedded may wonder how a Case Model 65 Loader could have 'sentimental value'. But Neil 'used to assemble them for the agents', so he's hanging on to his. Plus the turnip ridger and some drays. They're all 'on the restoration list, if I live long enough'.

He probably will, provided enjoyment is the key. Because Neil's having the time of his life. He's got heaps to do and room to do it. When he sold the farm and moved to town, the plan was to have a shed at home. But 'the council are so bloody minded. You can't have one high enough for a pygmy without special permission.' So he bought the warehouse instead.

'I've got no other interest,' says Neil. 'I'm not old enough for bowls or golf.' He's always 'enjoyed the mechanical side greatly. I like the satisfaction of doing it myself.' Which he does, for eight to ten hours a day. 'The privacy's important,' he says. 'I'll give cobbers a hand, but I'm a bit of a loner.'

One room here is what Neil calls 'the nerve centre, where I do the actual rebuilding'. Tools include a Colchester lathe, drill mill and metal-cutting band saw. Neil's already restored a number of Nortons, an old Chevy 4 x 4 and a cast-iron Fordson tractor. There are more bikes and two GMC trucks awaiting restoration. And a couple of rarities too. One's a 6-ton army surplus alternator that he used as a stand-by plant on the farm. The other's 'a self-loading Anderson concrete mixer. The motor and mixer bowl were made in Christchurch. It's quite unique, that. It did all the building on the farm.'

Of late, Neil's installed a sizable clock. 'I can be a bit erratic in my time going home,' he explains. But he's also adamant that 'this is not an escape. I've been married for forty-four years and I'd be quite happy if it was another forty-four. I think she escapes from me more than I from her. Your greatest wealth is your family. It's got to be.' That's why he hopes 'the boys will carry on the farming legacy when I have to stop. But they'll get a bike from Dad – that's the least I could do.'

Dave

Everything expands to fill the space

Teaching could never be called a tranquil craft. It's hard work and hard work and noisy to boot. For Dave, then, his shed's a necessary antidote to the hubbub and crowds at school. 'It's good to come out here and turn off,' he says. 'I like company, but you need the balance.'

The shed Dave unwinds in was built by his father. It is by no means the only one here. 'I don't know how many there are,' says Dave, 'but we're not short of them.'

A guided tour proves the point. We inspect the old, match-lined Post Office, brought onto the property as a barn. Behind it, an ageing implement shed where Dave's brother-in-law's two-seat trike with the big Chev motor is stored, and a Jeffery truck, one of two left in New Zealand. Elsewhere, more sheds store 'antique equipment and collectables'. Dave inspects an old sofa he plans to restore. 'Everything expands to fill the space,' he says. 'There's not enough time in the day.'

Especially since he devotes a good many hours to his traction engines and road locomotives. He's got two McLarens, a 1902 Model M and a 1913 Double Cranker, plus a 1912 Burrell. 'They'd pull 300 to 400 bales of wool,' Dave says. There's also a 100-year-old Anderson's threshing mill, 'still in working order'. After three generations 'nothing goes here. Everything stays on the property.'

The traction engines surely will. 'Steam gets in your bloodstream – the smell of it, the sound of it. But I'm not like some – who sleep in the boiler. I enjoy them but I'm not obsessed.' Perhaps not, but they do keep him busy. The workshop shed's equipped with an anvil and forge and a lovely old Dean Smith and Grace 2-ton lathe, 'the same as they fitted to ships in the old days'.

Teaching and toiling mean Dave doesn't get to bed very early. 'I'm often up at 2 a.m. doing school work.' Even so, he can't see the restoration work stopping. 'I don't think about the why of it all. My father spent his life here. I inherited a lot of it. I've seen it being restored by my father. I'm just following through, continuing a family tradition.'

Alan

It'd be lovely if it could all carry on

Everything in 'the den' tells a story. Like the golliwog Alan defiantly added to his 'little home museum' when they were 'banned for a while'. Or the candle, here as a reminder of life as a kid on the farm. 'We were peasants,' says Alan. 'The electricity broke down with monotonous regularity. The candle was our emergency power supply. There wasn't one in each room – just one candle!'

If the candle is significant, so are his restored walk-behind garden tractors. He's got a 1930s Kincad, very similar to the one he pushed as a boy. The Kincad's engine is in the middle of its single wheel 'so you get all the weight for traction. It's amazingly strong.' Alan proudly points out that the 4-stroke motor, with its automatic inlet valve and horseshoe magneto, 'still goes every time'.

Garden tractors may not seem the stuff of childhood, but 'we were pretty poor', says Alan. 'When I was a kid I thought shops were places in town where you just looked through the windows at things.' He thinks the pleasure he gets 'mucking round with old things' grew from the need to make what he couldn't

buy. But that's had its advantages, as when he wanted 'a decor anvil'. Since it was 'too costly to buy one', he scaled up a souvenir model, cut the sections from sheet steel and filled the structure with concrete to produce his own 'forged' anvil. There's even a manufacturer's name stamped on the side, to make sure 'it looks the part'.

Over the years, Alan's original small garage has done a Topsy. As well as the den, he's got a machine shop, an attic and room to restore his three Morris Minors. 'I don't like the saloons or lorries, but take the lid off – that's the convertible – and I love them.' He'll bequeath one convertible, but what saddens Alan is that he can see most of the history he's hung on to just slipping away.

'It'd be lovely if it could all carry on when I'm not around . . . but I don't think it will. There'll be a bloody auction and out it will go. I don't like the thought of that, but there you are . . .'

One thing's for sure. He's going to make the most of it while he's here.

Jim Hopkins Author

It has been said that, at some stage, everyone should plant a tree, build a house and write a book. If so, Jim Hopkins has, at least, managed two and a half of the Big Three. The tree's in, the book's finished (you're holding it) and although he hasn't built a house, he has built a shed. Even if the door's not in yet, nor the big window, cunningly planned to encourage the growth of seedlings. While it doesn't compare with the greats in this volume, his still incomplete shed maintains a link with those fabled structures that goes right back to his urchin days.

He still remembers the four sheds dotted around the sprawling section at home, and the one in a corner of the South Intermediate playground, filled with ancient printing presses and equipment by an enthusiastic teacher. For years, he has stupefied anyone foolish enough to listen with tales of the Vulcan that flew over the woodwork room (which is really a learning shed). Or with needlessly detailed accounts of his exploits as an ATC cadet lost in a vast hangar (which is really a shed for things with wings). Since then, sadly, his shed credentials have languished somewhat, although as soon as the door's fitted that will change. The fact of the matter is he's spent far too much time making speeches, doing debates and immersing himself in the lurid precincts of radio and television studios (which are really sheds for people with exhibitionist tendencies). It is to be hoped that working on this book will have shown him the error of his ways.

Julie Riley Photographer

Astronaut, dancer, brain surgeon, prop. These are just some of the people Julie Riley has photographed in a career that has spanned the pages of major newspapers, leading magazines and, more recently, two books of her own. The first of these, *Men Alone*, examined solitary lives in remote places. With an unerring eye that has been said to 'catch details even the Hubble telescope would miss', Julie's images captured special people in special places. So did her second book, *Our Town*, an evocative look at the small centres and hamlets that give New Zealand so much of its character (and contain so many of its finest sheds). Indeed, to Julie goes the honour of providing the inspiration for the title of this book, originally suggesting it be called *Men Alone in Our Town out the Back in*

their Sheds. At one stage it was proposed the cover be adapted to also serve as a metre rule, which could incorporate this title, but tragically, the accountants stepped in.

A fearless adventurer, Julie has, so far, built a shed and co-built an entire house. She's also one of the few Kiwis who has actually been a fish farmer, and still describes the muster as the hardest part. In between times, she's learnt to fly in a week. (And then to fly in a plane.) A keen yachtie and climber, she today has not one but two sheds to retreat to when the need arises. During the week she heads the professional photography course in the Art and Design Department at Christchurch Polytechnic (which is really a shed for the head).

A second volume of **Blokes and Sheds** is currently being planned. If you have an interesting shed, or know of someone who has one, please write to:

The Editor
HarperCollins Publishers
P.O.Box 1
Auckland